Contents

Features

The *Word Problem Practice* series offers parents and educators a unique way to teach foundational math concepts in a way that students will truly enjoy. *Word Problem Practice* involves students in real-life, high-interest word problems that they will want to solve.

The components of each *Word Problem Practice* page are:

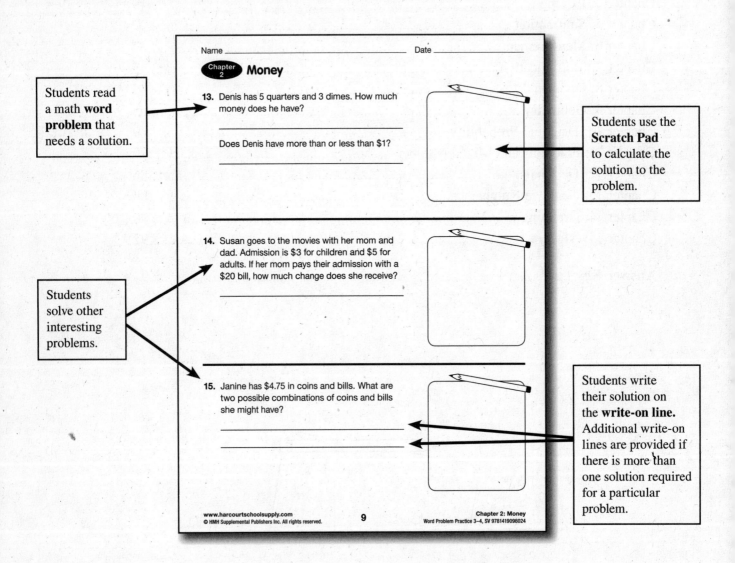

Students read a math **word problem** that needs a solution.

Students use the **Scratch Pad** to calculate the solution to the problem.

Students solve other interesting problems.

Students write their solution on the **write-on line.** Additional write-on lines are provided if there is more than one solution required for a particular problem.

Name _____ Date _____

Chapter 2 **Money**

13. Denis has 5 quarters and 3 dimes. How much money does he have?

_____

Does Denis have more than or less than $1?

_____

14. Susan goes to the movies with her mom and dad. Admission is $3 for children and $5 for adults. If her mom pays their admission with a $20 bill, how much change does she receive?

_____

15. Janine has $4.75 in coins and bills. What are two possible combinations of coins and bills she might have?

_____

_____

9

Chapter 2: Money
Word Problem Practice 3–4, SV 9781419098024

Finally, an **Answer Key** is included so students, parents, and teachers can check to make sure the answers to all the problems are correct.

Chapter 1 **Place Value**

1. Which addition problem has a sum that is farthest to the left on a number line?

   4,286 + 9,184 or 8,725 + 5,296

   _____

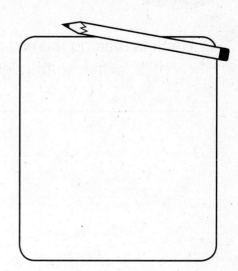

2. How many different three-digit numbers can be formed from the digits 7, 8, and 9, using each digit exactly once?

   _____

   Write the numbers.

   _____

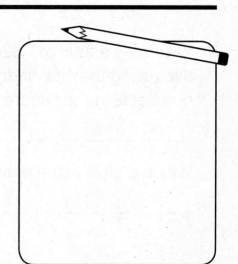

3. A class collected used paperback books for a sale. Brenda donated 18 books, Kyle donated 15, Leesa donated 21, and Neil donated 19. Who donated the greatest number of books?

   _____

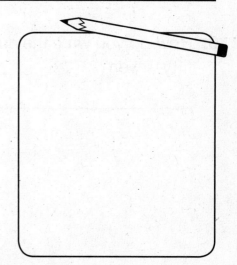

Chapter 1 — Place Value

4. Hank is making a time line. Does he place 1962 or 1978 farther to the right on the time line?

_____

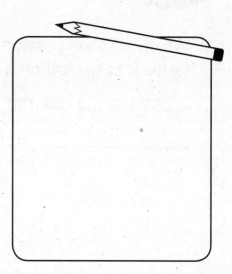

5. Yesterday a total of 1,826 cars crossed the river using the new bridge. Which digit in this number is in the hundreds place?

_____

Which digit is in the ones place?

_____

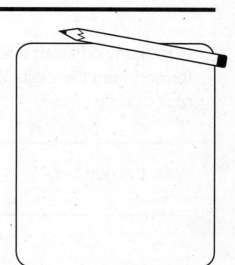

6. How do you write the number sixty thousand fifty-seven?

_____

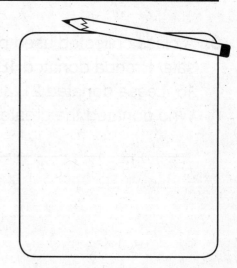

Chapter 2 Money

1. Sarah and Mark each have $1.00. Sarah buys an ice-cream cone for 69 cents, and Mark buys a snow cone for 55 cents. Who has more change left?

_____

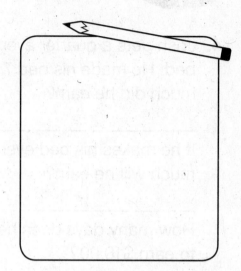

2. Krista has a pocketful of coins. She reaches in and pulls out 7 dimes. How much money does she have?

_____

She pulls out 6 more dimes. What is the total now?

_____

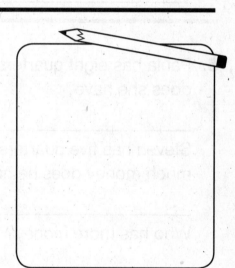

3. Pat says that a jacket costs about $28. Assume that she rounds the cost to the nearest dollar. What are the least and the most the jacket can cost?

_____

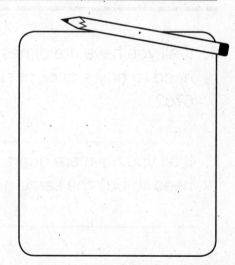

Chapter 2 **Money**

4. Josh gets a quarter every time he makes his bed. He made his bed 7 days in a row. How much did he earn?

_____

If he makes his bed every day for 30 days, how much will he earn?

_____

How many days does he have to make his bed to earn $10.00?

_____

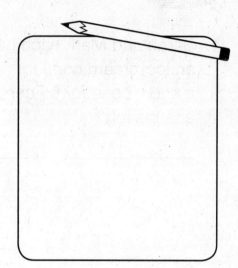

5. Paula has eight quarters. How much money does she have?

_____

Steven has five quarters and 7 nickels. How much money does he have?

_____

Who has more money?

_____

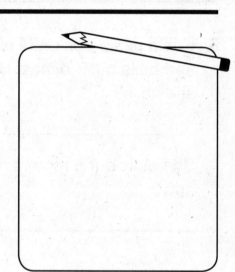

6. If all you have are dimes, how many do you need to buy a pack of shoelaces that costs 67¢?

_____

If all you have are quarters, how many do you need to buy the same pack of shoelaces?

_____

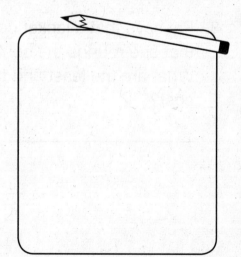

Name _____   Date _____

7. Francine wants to buy a toy that costs $2.50. She has one $5 bill and two $1 bills. Which bills should she use to pay for the toy?

_____

How much change should she receive?

_____

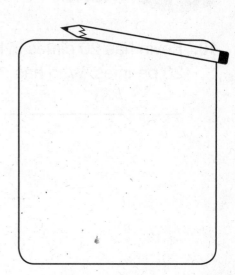

8. Gilberto purchases school supplies that cost a total of $39.25. If Gilberto pays the clerk $50.00, about how much change does he get?

_____

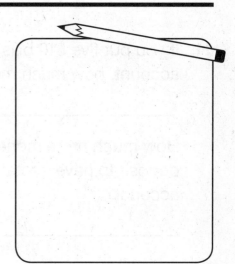

9. Stephanie purchases a gallon of milk for $2.65. She pays with a $5 bill. How much change does she receive?

_____

Does she have enough change to buy another gallon of milk?

_____

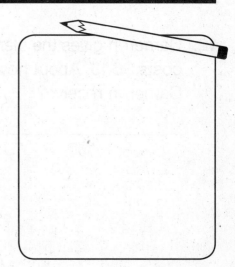

Name _____   Date _____

10. Kevin has 20 dimes in his pocket. Carrie has 20 pennies. Who has more money?

_____

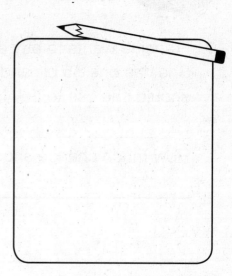

11. If you put five $10 bills into a new savings account, how much money do you deposit?

_____

How much more money do you need to deposit to have a total of $100 in your savings account?

_____

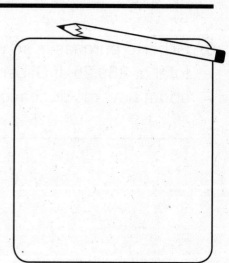

12. Cameron gives the clerk $10 for a poster that costs $6.15. About how much change does Cameron receive?

_____

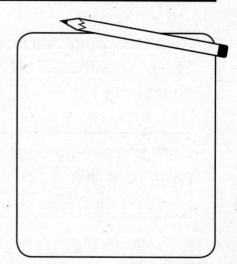

Name _____ Date _____

13. Denis has 5 quarters and 3 dimes. How much money does he have?

_____

Does Denis have more than or less than $1?

_____

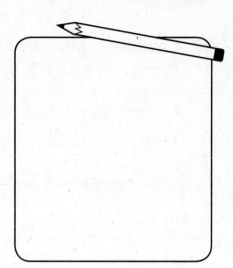

---

14. Susan goes to the movies with her mom and dad. Admission is $3 for children and $5 for adults. If her mom pays their admission with a $20 bill, how much change does she receive?

_____

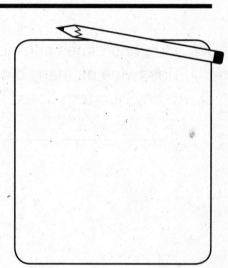

---

15. Janine has $4.75 in coins and bills. What are two possible combinations of coins and bills she might have?

_____

_____

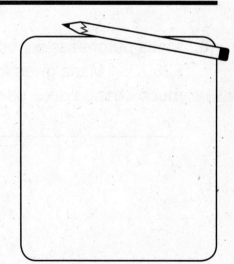

Name _____ Date _____

16. Last week, Ms. Larkins earned $354. Mrs. Wong earned $476. Who earned more money?

_____

How much more did that person earn?

_____

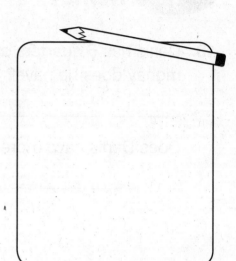

17. Bob has dimes and quarters totaling $2.25. He has twice as many dimes as quarters. How many quarters does Bob have?

_____

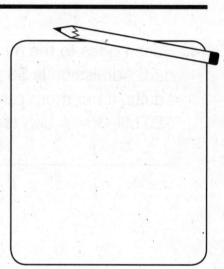

18. Maria purchases school supplies that cost $28.75. If Maria gives the clerk $40, about how much change does she receive?

_____

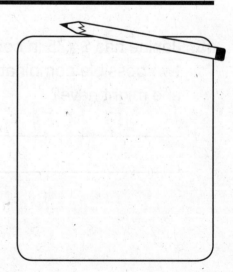

Name _____   Date _____

19. What amount is double $19.32?

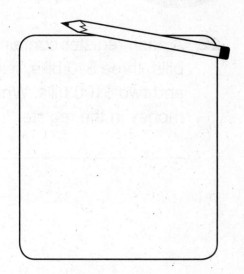

_____

20. Estimate the difference.

$119.95 − $74.50

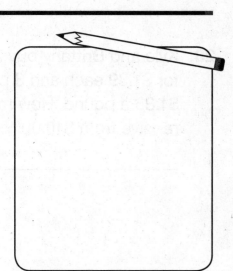

_____

21. Grace and Kris go to the zoo with their moms.
All 4 buy souvenirs. Grace and Kris each buy
1 pencil and 1 pair of sunglasses. Their
mothers each get 1 key chain. Pencils cost
$1.00, sunglasses are $2.00, and key chains
are $4.00. How much do they spend
altogether?

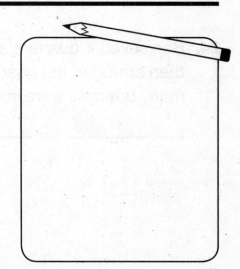

_____

Chapter 2 Money

22. A cash register contains these bills: four $1 bills, three $10 bills, two $20 bills, one $50 bill, and two $100 bills. What is the total amount of money in the register?

_____

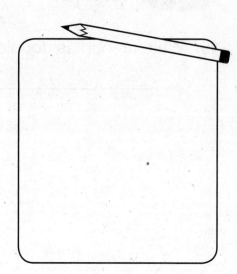

23. Kyle and Brittany buy 2 quarts of blueberries for $1.39 each and 3 pounds of tomatoes for $1.35 a pound. How much change do they receive from $10.00?

_____

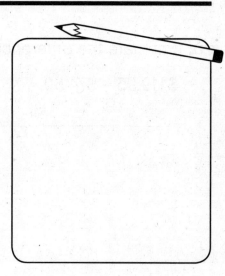

24. Ben saved 4 quarters each day for 1 week. He then arranged the quarters in 4 piles. How many quarters were in each pile?

_____

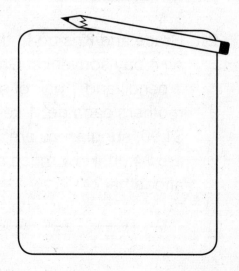

Chapter 2 **Money**

25. Each day at school, Tran buys a $0.70 glass of juice in the cafeteria. If he was not absent from school last week, how much did Tran spend on juice for the week?

_____

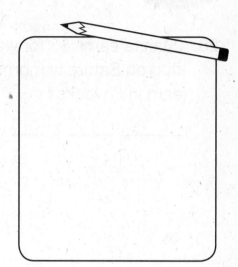

26. Tom, Dana, Jerri, and Alan want to share $1 equally. How much money should each person receive?

_____

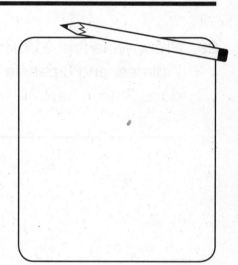

27. A jar of paste costs $0.84, and a book of construction paper is $0.99. Nickie needs 2 jars of paste and 3 books of construction paper. She has $5.00. Does she have enough money?

_____

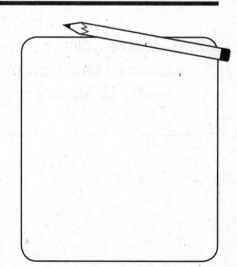

Name _____ Date _____

28. Juanita earns $3 for walking her neighbor's dog on Saturday mornings. How much will she earn in 5 weeks?

_____

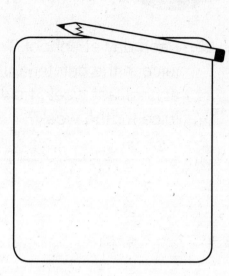

29. Shawn has four $1 bills, 4 half-dollars, 2 dimes, and 8 pennies. How much money does Shawn have?

_____

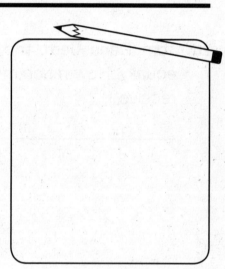

30. A local recycling company will pay 2 cents per aluminum can. How much will Joshua earn if he sells 60 aluminum cans?

_____

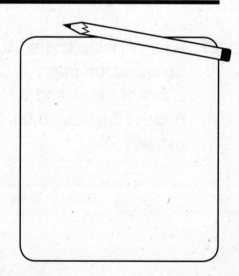

Name _____   Date _____

Chapter 3 **Time**

1. Margie studied for one-third hour. How many minutes is this?

_____

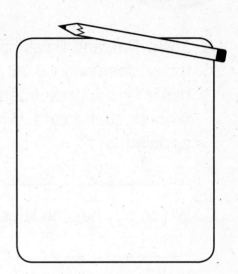

2. In 24-hour time, the hours are numbered from 0 to 2400. For example, midnight is 0 hours and noon is 1200 hours. Therefore, 1300 hours is 13 hours after midnight or 1:00 P.M. What time is 1600 hours?

_____

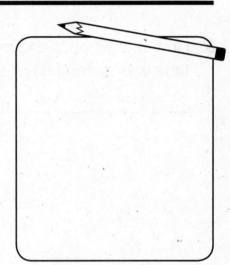

3. Northbound trains arrive at a train station every 20 minutes, and southbound trains arrive every 30 minutes. A northbound train and a southbound train arrive at 6:00 A.M. How many trains arrive at the station at 6:30 A.M.?

_____

How many trains arrive at the station at 7:00 A.M.?

_____

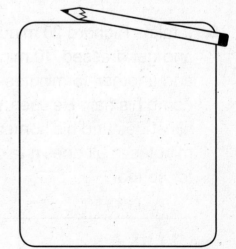

Chapter 3 **Time**

4. Josh, Tim, and Palak have dentist appointments today. Josh has a 9:00 A.M. appointment. Palak has a 1 P.M. appointment. Tim's appointment is 6 hours after Josh's. What time is Tim's appointment?

_____

Which boy has the latest appointment?

_____

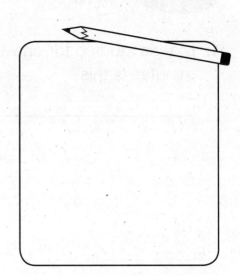

5. How many hours and minutes elapse from the time your school day begins to the time it ends?

_____

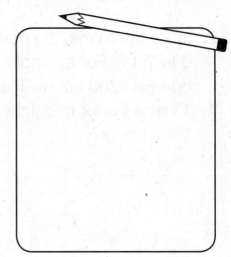

6. It takes Richard 20 minutes to get out of bed and get dressed, 10 minutes to eat breakfast, and another 15 minutes to brush his teeth and comb his hair. He uses 10 minutes more to find his shoes and his homework. How many minutes in all does it take Richard to get ready for school?

_____

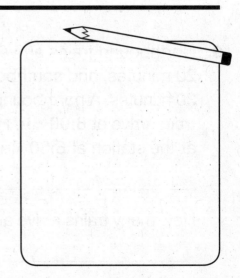

Chapter 3 **Time**

7. Olivia is going to a party that starts at 5:00 P.M. It takes 25 minutes to get to the party. At what time should Olivia leave for the party if she wants to arrive at exactly 5:00 P.M.?

_____

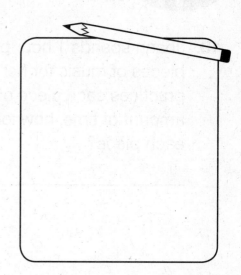

8. Janie and her friend are taking turns on the big slide. It takes them about 2 minutes to both get a turn. About how many times can Janie slide in half an hour?

_____

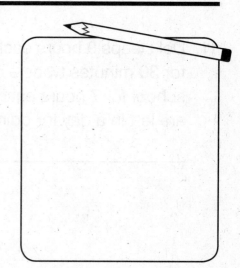

9.

April						
Sunday	Monday	Tuesday	Wednesday	Thursday	Friday	Saturday
				1	2	3
4	5	6	7	8	9	10
11	12	13	14	15	16	17
18	19	20	21	22	23	24
25	26	27	28	29	30	

Look at the calendar. The robotics class takes a two-week break beginning April 14. On what day and date do classes begin again?

_____

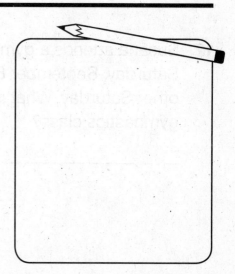

Chapter 3 **Time**

10. Joann spends 1 hour practicing 5 different pieces of music for her recital. If Joann practices each piece of music the same amount of time, how long does she practice each piece?

_____

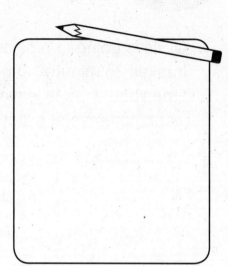

11. Del sleeps 9 hours each day and walks his dog for 30 minutes twice a day. If Del is also in school for 7 hours each day, how many hours are left in a day for doing other things?

_____

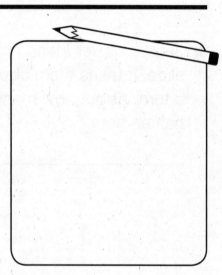

12. Susana attends a gymnastics class on Saturday, September 8. The class meets every other Saturday. What is the date of the next gymnastics class?

_____

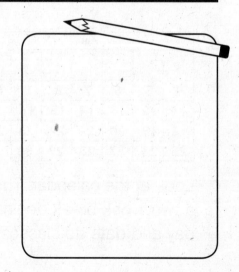

Name _____ Date _____

1. What is the smallest 2-digit number in which the sum of the digits is 7?

_____

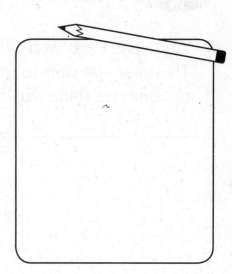

2. Two students brought cookies to school for a class party. Tami brought 46 cookies, and Liz brought 27 cookies. What is the total number of cookies the girls brought?

_____

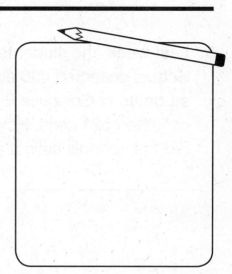

3. Bob has 24 fishing lures. His father gives him 12 more. Then Bob buys 2 more lures at a garage sale. Now how many lures does Bob have?

_____

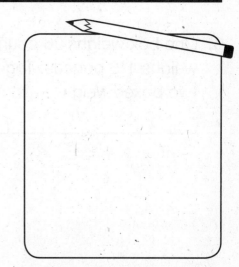

Chapter 4 **Addition**

4. Last year, Perla won 14 ribbons at a horse show. This year she won 18 more ribbons. How many ribbons has Perla won over the 2-year period?

_____

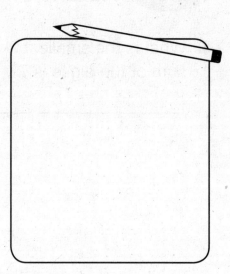

5. Last week, the students at Addams Elementary School collected 436 aluminum cans, and the students at Gonzales Elementary School collected 521 cans. How many aluminum cans did the schools collect altogether?

_____

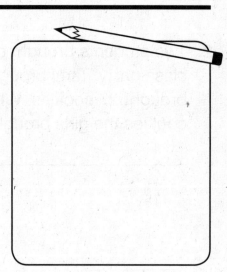

6. One box weighs 96 pounds. Another box weighs 115 pounds. Together, how much do the two boxes weigh?

_____

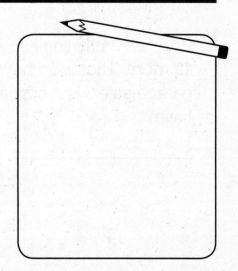

Chapter 4 **Addition**

7. To get home from school, Brianna walks 3 blocks south, 2 blocks east, and 1 more block south. How far does she walk in all?

_____

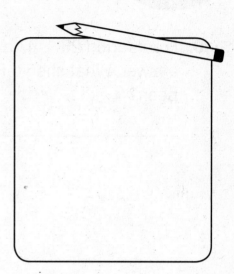

8. Three children are running in a relay race. It is 50 yards from the starting line to the first handoff. It is 75 yards from the first handoff to the second handoff. It is 100 yards from the second handoff to the finish line. How far is it from the starting line to the finish line?

_____

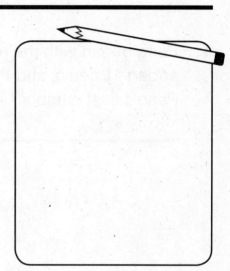

9. Sheila wants to know how many electrical outlets are in her home. She counts 8 outlets in the basement, 14 on the lower level, and 12 on the upper level. She also sees 1 outlet on the stairway. How many outlets does she find?

_____

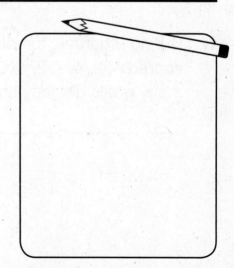

Chapter 4 **Addition**

10. Fran added 23 + 47 and wrote 60 as her answer. What should Fran's answer have been?

_____

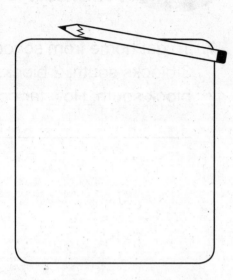

11. Pang began with the number 12, added 11, added 11 again, and then added 13. What was Pang's final number?

_____

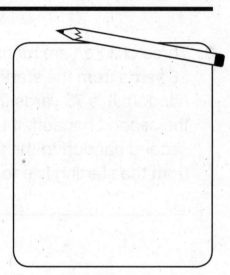

12. During 9 games, the players in a hockey club scored 4, 2, 4, 7, 2, 4, 0, 6, and 8 goals. How many goals did they score in all?

_____

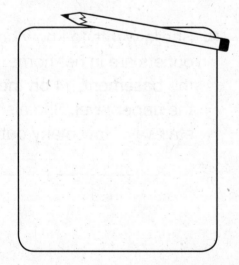

Chapter 4 **Addition**

13. A stadium has 37,834 reserved seats and 11,684 bleacher seats. Estimate the seating capacity by rounding each number to the nearest thousand.

_____

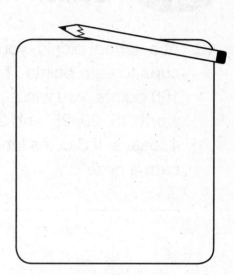

14. Washington has 3,026 miles of shoreline along the Pacific Ocean. Its neighboring state, Oregon, has 1,410 miles of shoreline. Together, how many miles of shoreline do the two states have along the Pacific Ocean?

_____

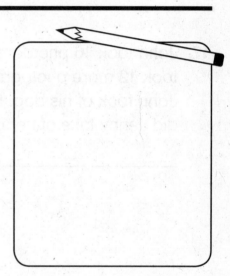

15. Bridget is 5 years older than her sister. If Bridget's sister is 16 years old, how old is Bridget?

_____

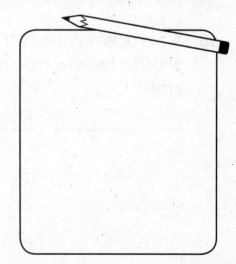

16. At a school picnic, you can toss coins into cups to earn points. If you earn exactly 100 points, you win a prize. The cups are worth 15, 20, 25, and 30 points. Ben makes 4 tosses. If 3 coins land in cups, does he earn a prize?

_____

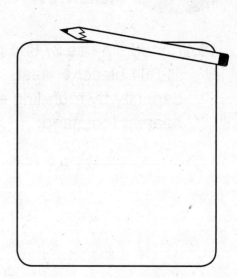

17. John took 16 photographs of his dog. Jenny took 12 more photographs of her cat than John took of his dog. How many photographs did Jenny take of her cat?

_____

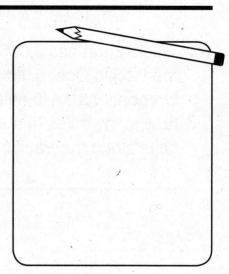

18. A biologist banded 218 mallards, 394 geese, and 751 herons. How many birds did she band in all?

_____

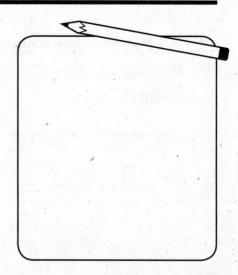

Chapter 4 Addition

19. The students at a school collected 7,109 cans, 8,342 glass bottles, and 7,957 plastic bottles. How many items did they collect in all?

_____

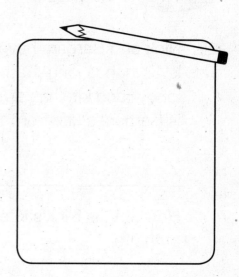

20. In 1926, two men traveled around the world in less than 29 days. They traveled 4,110 miles by train and car, about 6,300 miles by plane, and about 8,000 miles by ship. About how far did they travel in all?

_____

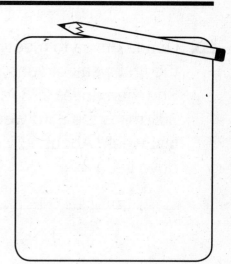

21. Mr. Tovar drove 6 miles to the store. Then he drove 5 miles to the library. He went from the library to the gas station, which was another 3 miles. He drove 2 miles to the bank. Then he drove 11 miles to get home. How many miles did Mr. Tovar drive in all?

_____

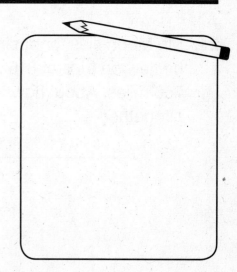

Chapter 4 Addition

22. Nick and Barbara have new kites. Nick's kite is 12 inches long. Barbara's kite is 9 inches long. Each kite has an 8-inch tail. How long is Barbara's kite from the top to the end of the tail?

_____

How long is Nick's kite from the top to the end of the tail?

_____

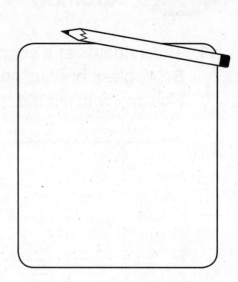

23. Donna drives to meetings each week. During the first week of June, she drives 196 miles. She then drives 273 miles the second week, 301 miles the third week, and 283 miles the last week. About how many miles does Donna drive in June?

_____

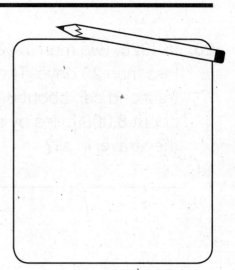

24. Mr. Moon flies for business trips. Last week he flew on trips of 816 miles, 423 miles, and 768 miles. About how far did Mr. Moon fly altogether?

_____

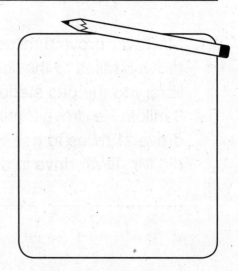

Chapter 5 **Subtraction**

1. I am less than 55. I am greater than 49. Subtract my digits, and you'll get 3. What number am I?

_____

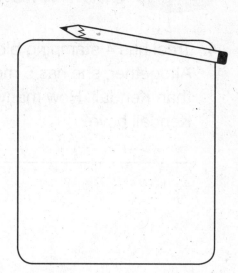

2. Emilio, Kari, and Alicia are having a reading contest. The person who reads the most chapters in 4 weeks wins. Emilio reads 19 chapters the first week. Then he reads 7 chapters during each remaining week. Kari reads 7 chapters every week. Alicia reads 12 chapters the first week, 3 the second, none the third, and 6 the fourth. How many more chapters does Emilio read than Alicia?

_____

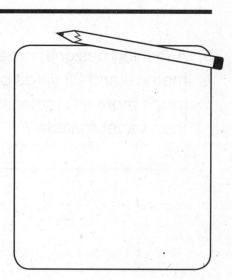

3. Joshua has 4 sweaters in one drawer. He has 3 fewer sweaters in another drawer. How many sweaters does Joshua have altogether?

_____

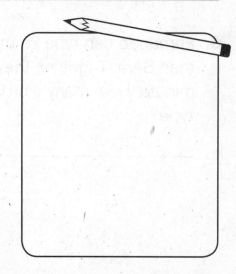

Chapter 5 **Subtraction**

4. Traci has 4 stamping blocks. She buys 8 more. Altogether, she has 5 more stamping blocks than Kendall. How many stamping blocks does Kendall have?

_____

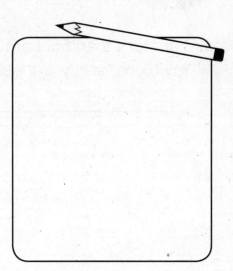

5. A fashion designer orders 24 yards of velvet material and 32 yards of silk material. How much more silk material does the designer order than velvet material?

_____

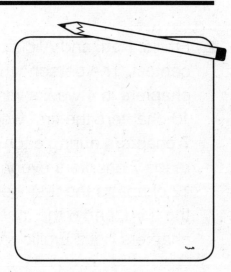

6. Fernando can type 25 more words per minute than Sara. Together, they type 135 words per minute. How many words per minute does Sara type?

_____

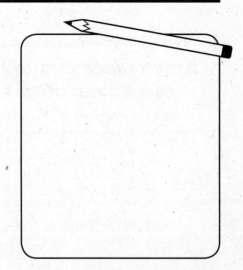

Chapter 5 **Subtraction**

7. Kayla has 23 seashells and finds 28 more. Randy has 31 seashells and finds 18 more. Who has the greater number of seashells?

_____

How many more seashells does that person have?

_____

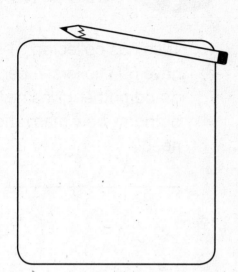

8. Stephen counts 238 pennies in his coin bank. Stephanie counts 149 pennies in her coin bank. How many more pennies does Stephen have?

_____

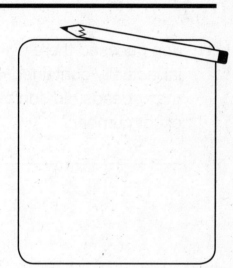

9. Anthony has 137 pennies. His sister Tonika has 216 pennies. Their mother has 418 pennies. If Anthony and Tonika put their pennies together, how many pennies fewer or how many pennies more do they have than their mother?

_____

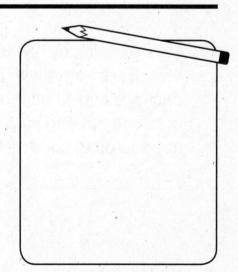

Chapter 5 Subtraction

10. Trish has collected 31 stickers. She wants to have 50 stickers in her collection. If her grandmother gives her 10 stickers for her birthday, how many more stickers does she need?

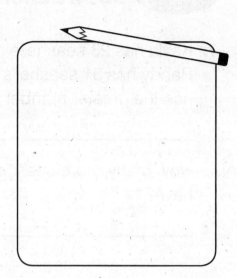

_____

11. Jon guessed there were 317 beads in a jar. The jar actually contained 429 beads. By how many beads did Jon's guess differ from the exact number?

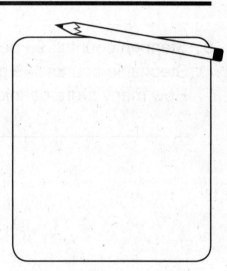

_____

12. Mr. Rolle already has 8 hot dog buns. Then he buys 2 packages with 8 hot dog buns in each package and 12 beef hot dogs. If Mr. Rolle puts one hot dog in each bun, how many extra hot dog buns does he have?

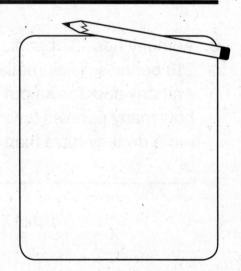

_____

Chapter 5 **Subtraction**

13. Three people are celebrating birthdays. Ms. Estrada is 7 years younger than Mr. Jung but 3 years older than Mrs. Nelson. Mr. Jung is 42. How old are Ms. Estrada and Mrs. Nelson?

Ms. Estrada: _____

Mrs. Nelson: _____

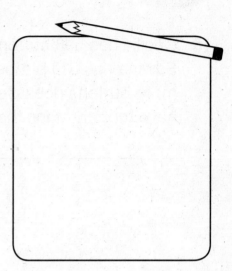

14. A plane took off from Sacramento with 108 people aboard. When it landed in Los Angeles, 59 people got off and 137 got on. How many people were on the plane when it left Los Angeles?

_____

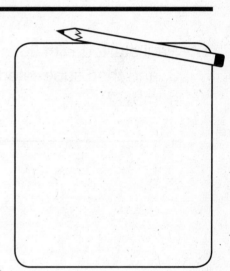

15. A school is collecting cans for a food drive. The goal is 300 cans. First grade students bring in 99 cans. Second grade students bring in 96 cans. Third grade students bring in 102 cans. How many more cans are needed?

_____

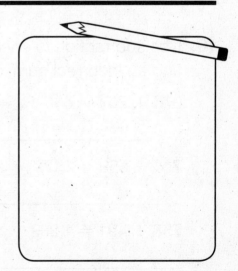

Chapter 5 **Subtraction**

16. Cecilia has 598 buttons in her collection. Edwina has 619 buttons in hers. How many more buttons does Cecilia need in order to have more buttons than Edwina?

_____

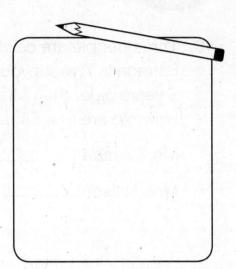

---

17. Paul started with 36, subtracted 2, subtracted 3, and then subtracted 5. What was Paul's final number?

_____

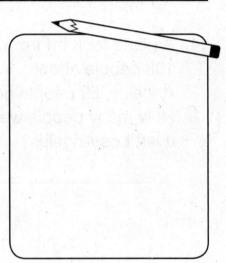

---

18. Use subtraction to check these sums. If you find an incorrect sum, correct it.

$376 + 267 = 643$

_____

$714 + 559 = 1,173$

_____

$758 + 491 = 1,289$

_____

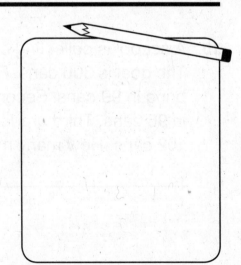

Chapter 5 **Subtraction**

19. At a local farm, Robin collected 24 white eggs and 27 brown eggs, while Andrea collected 42 white eggs and 39 brown eggs. On the way home, 13 of the eggs were broken. How many eggs did the girls have that were not broken?

_____

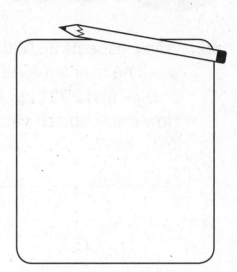

20. Mr. Cooper has 70,000 frequent-flyer miles. He uses 25,000 miles for a trip to Seattle and 18,000 miles for a trip to Palm Springs. Does he have enough frequent-flyer miles left to take a trip that is 28,000 miles long?

_____

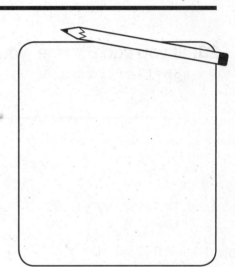

21. If you start with 8, add 23, subtract 15, and subtract 9, what number do you end up with?

_____

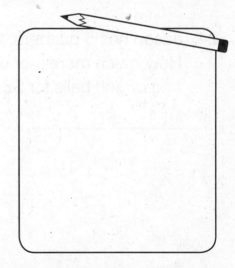

33

Chapter 5 **Subtraction**

22. Frank inspects 36,000 apples every week. Last week he rejected 1,796 apples because of bruises and 2,731 apples because of worms. How many apples passed Frank's inspection last week?

_____

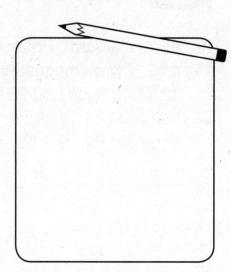

23. If you add 6 to me, you get 25. What number am I?

_____

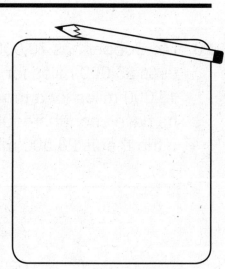

24. Jason has 5 quarters, 2 dimes, and a $5 bill. How much more money does he need to buy a bag of golf balls for $6.49?

_____

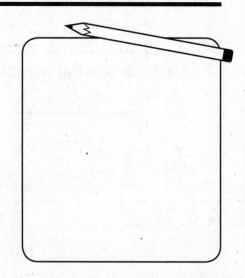

Chapter 5 Subtraction

25. A car on parade in the year 2000 was made in 1925. How old was the car at the time of the parade?

_____

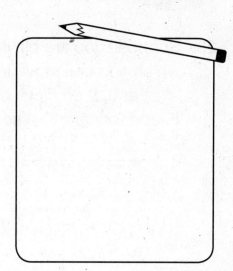

26. The sum of 3 numbers is 500. Two of the numbers are 215 and 138. What is the third number?

_____

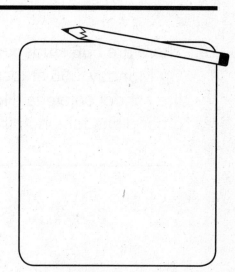

27. Suppose you are playing a board game in which you can move forward or backward. You start at 3, then move forward 3, back 6, and forward 7. Where are you then?

_____

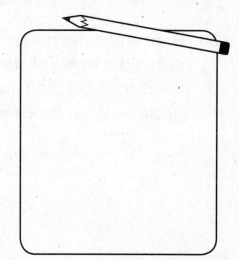

Chapter 5 **Subtraction**

28. Suppose you are playing a board game in which you can move forward or backward. You start at 0, then move back 4, forward 6, back 8, and forward 3. Where are you then?

_____

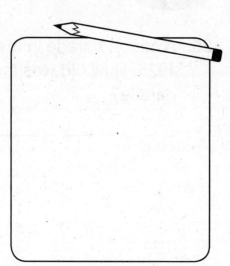

29. There are 536 students in City Grade School. On Monday, 396 students bring their lunch to the school cafeteria. How many students have other plans for lunch that day?

_____

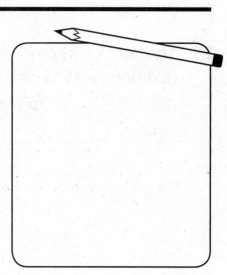

30. Brad entered a stairwell on the 5th floor. He climbed 8 flights of stairs, delivered a package to his manager, and then went down 3 flights of stairs. What floor was Brad on at that time?

_____

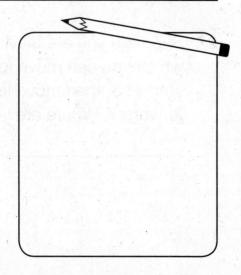

Name _____   Date _____

1. Choose an object in your classroom, and then use a ruler to measure the length of that object to the nearest inch. Which object did you choose?

   _____

   How long is the object measured to the nearest inch?

   _____

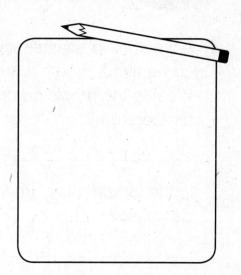

2. If you know that it takes 2 full paper cups of water to fill 1 mug, how many full paper cups of water does it take to fill 2 mugs?

   _____

   How many full cups of water does it take to fill 4 mugs?

   _____

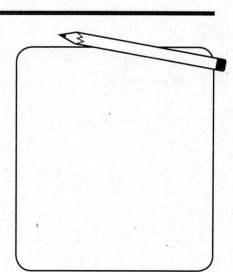

3. The fuel tank of an automobile can hold 11 gallons of gasoline. The last time the tank was filled, 42 quarts of gasoline were put in the tank. How much gasoline was in the tank before it was filled?

   _____

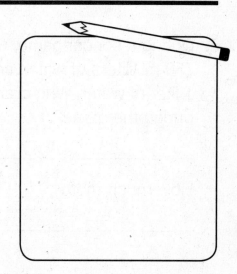

Chapter 6 **Measurement**

4. A weather forecaster says the temperature is currently 52°F, with a predicted high of 63°F. What is the predicted change in the temperature?

_____

Is the temperature predicted to increase or decrease?

_____

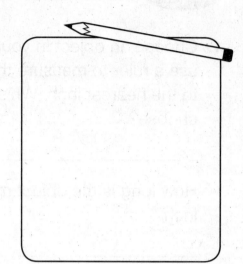

5. Does a 2-liter bottle or two 1-liter bottles hold more water?

_____

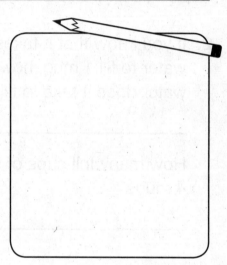

6. During a soccer game, Chantel drank 750 milliliters of water, and Kendra drank 1 liter of water. Who drank more water during the game?

_____

How much more?

_____

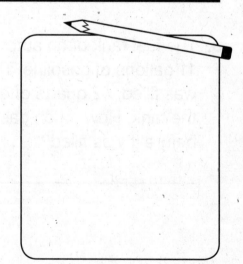

Chapter 6 **Measurement**

7. Suppose that the temperature outside was 32°F one hour ago. Since that time, the temperature has fallen 8°F. What is the temperature now?

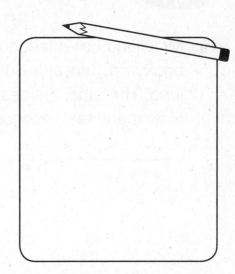

_____

8. Catrina has 30 ounces of orange juice. Does she have enough juice to fill four 8-ounce glasses?

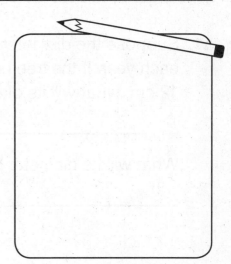

_____

9. Kim made punch for a party. She used 1 pint of grape juice, 4 cups of apple juice, and 1 quart of orange juice. How many cups of punch did Kim make?

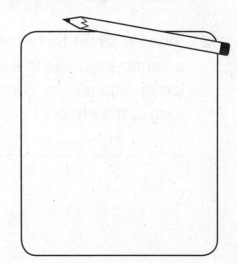

_____

Chapter 6 **Measurement**

10. Mr. Ching has a fenced dog pen in his backyard. Two sides of the pen are 6 feet long. The other 2 sides are 8 feet long. How many feet of fence are there in all?

_____

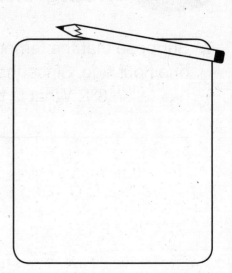

11. Suppose the diameter of a tree increases 3 cm each year. If the tree now has a diameter of 12 cm, what will its diameter be in 5 years?

_____

What will its diameter be in 20 years?

_____

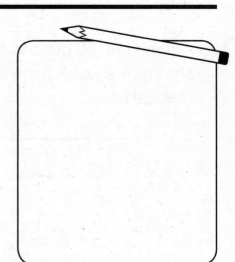

12. Along a street there are 6 lampposts. If there is a lamppost on each end of the street and the lampposts are spaced 150 feet apart, how long is the street?

_____

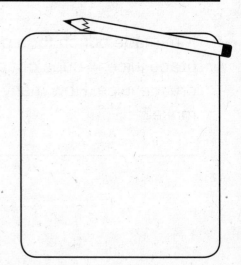

Chapter 6 **Measurement**

13. If 1 rice cake weighs 15 grams, how much do 5 rice cakes weigh?

_____

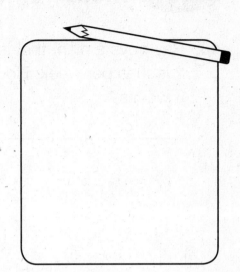

14. On Wednesday, the high temperature in Buffalo, New York, was 62°F and in Austin, Texas, it was 91°F. How much colder was the temperature in Buffalo?

_____

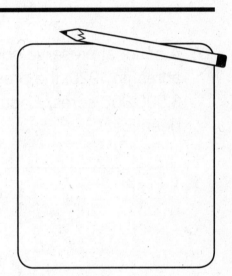

15. The start of a hiking path has an elevation of 583 feet. The path ends at an elevation of 1,874 feet. What is the change in elevation of the hiking path?

_____

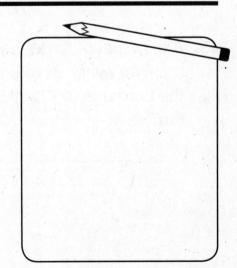

Chapter 6 **Measurement**

16. Ray buys a plant that is 1 inch tall. It grows 2 inches per week. How tall is the plant in 8 weeks?

_____

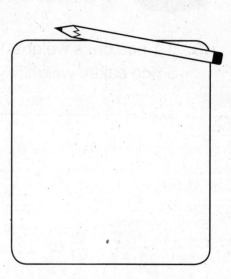

17. A national preserve covers nearly 300,000 acres. In 1920, the preserve covered nearly 3,500,000 acres. About how many acres have been lost?

_____

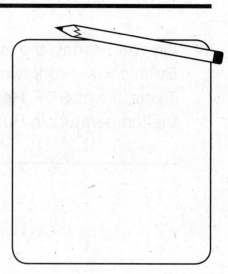

18. A brick patio border uses a pattern of 1 brown brick for every 2 tan bricks. The perimeter of the border is 327 bricks. How many bricks are tan?

_____

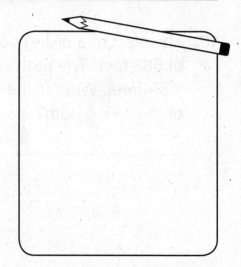

Chapter 6 **Measurement**

19. The same number represents both the perimeter and the area of a square. What is the length of 1 side of the square?

_____

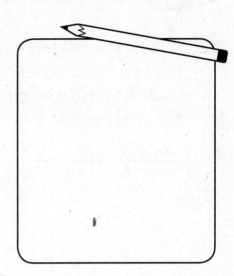

20. A rectangle is twice as long as it is wide. The area is 32 cm². What is the longest measure of the rectangle?

_____

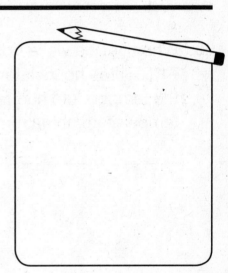

21. A diagonal of a rectangle creates 2 right triangles. How does the area of 1 right triangle compare to the area of the rectangle?

_____

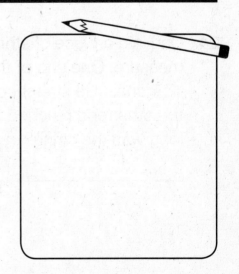

Chapter 6 **Measurement**

22. A cube that measures 3 inches on each side is inside another cube that measures 4 inches on each side. How much empty space is inside the larger cube?

_____

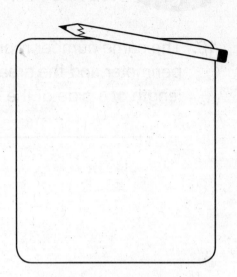

23. When Leticia woke up, the temperature was 71°F. Three hours later, a radio announcer said the temperature had fallen 12°F. What was the temperature at that time?

_____

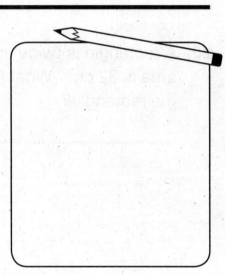

24. Carl laid a piece of string along a tape measure. One end of the string was at 17 inches. He stretched the string until the other end reached 54 inches. How long was the string?

_____

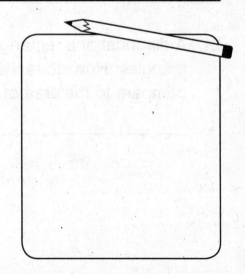

Chapter 7 Multiplication

1. Ryan has 8 boxes, each of which contains 10 water glasses. Meg has 7 boxes, each of which contains 10 water glasses. How many more water glasses does Ryan have than Meg?

_____

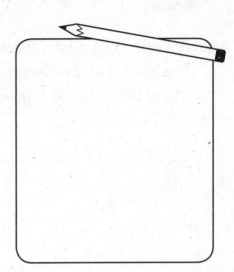

2. Suppose 4 erasers placed end to end equal the length of 1 new pencil. How many erasers would you have to place end to end to equal the length of 3 new pencils?

_____

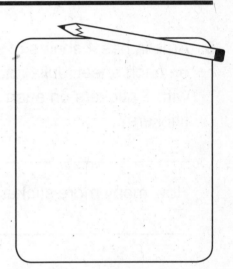

3. Movie tickets cost $5 each. How much does it cost for Pedro, Marcel, and Marie to see a movie?

_____

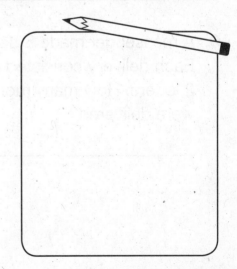

Chapter 7 **Multiplication**

4. Joseph built a bird feeder. Six birds each visit the feeder at 3 different times each day. How many times is the feeder visited by a bird each day?

_____

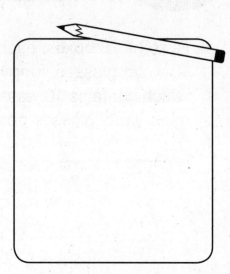

5. Amelia has 4 sheets of stickers with 5 stickers on each sheet. Julia has 3 sheets of stickers with 7 stickers on each sheet. Who has more stickers?

_____

How many more stickers?

_____

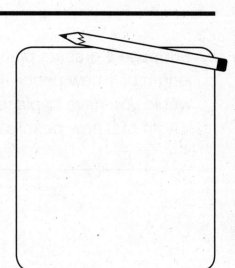

6. A messenger made 5 deliveries to a company. Each delivery consisted of 1 package and 2 letters. How many more letters than packages were delivered?

_____

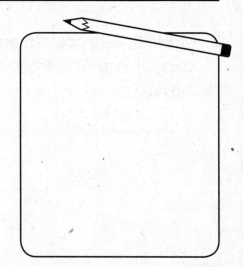

Chapter 7 **Multiplication**

7. There are 2 reading tables in the library. There are 10 chairs at each of these tables. How many students can sit at the reading tables?

_____

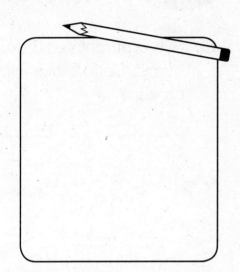

8. A librarian counted 5 storybooks on each of 3 shelves. Later she counted 5 more storybooks. How many storybooks did she count altogether?

_____

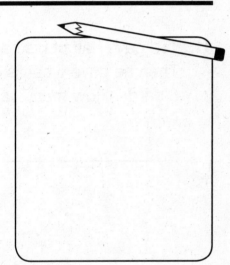

9. Lita and Patricia each have 3 packs of trading cards. Each pack contains 5 cards. How many trading cards do they have altogether?

_____

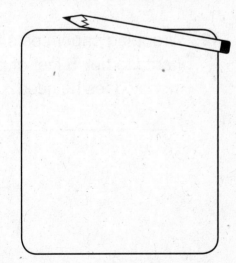

Chapter 7 **Multiplication**

10. Sylvie purchased 3 dozen eggs. On her way home, 1 egg broke. How many eggs were not broken?

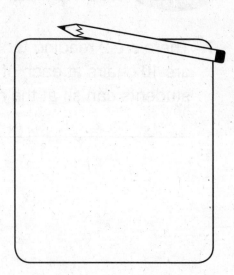

_____

11. Ted gave half of his baseball cards to Benito. Then he gave 5 cards to Dan. Now Ted has 6 cards. How many cards did he have to start with?

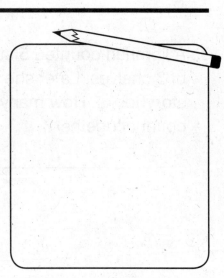

_____

12. Wrapping paper costs 20¢ per foot. Greg wants to buy 5 feet of paper. How much money does he need?

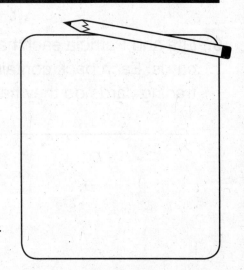

_____

Chapter 7 Multiplication

13. Carolyn wants to bring cookies to school in a tin box. She can fit 8 stacks of cookies in the box, with 5 cookies in each stack. How many cookies fit in the box altogether?

_____

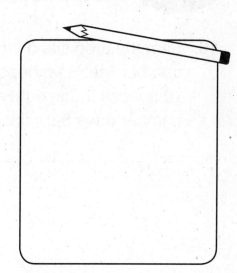

14. A building has 6 floors. If each floor has 8 windows, how many windows are there in the entire building?

_____

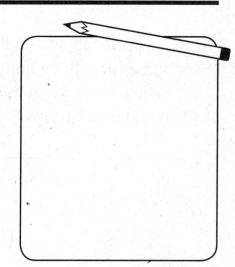

15. Gino and Tina have $4 each. They go to the store and see that perfume costs $14, flowers cost $8, and a wallet costs $10. Which gift can Gino and Tina afford to buy for their mom?

_____

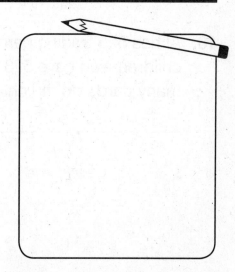

Chapter 7 **Multiplication**

16. Sam the Frog sits on the number 5 on a number line. Sam hops 6 times, moving 10 spaces to the right each time. On which number does Sam finally rest?

_____

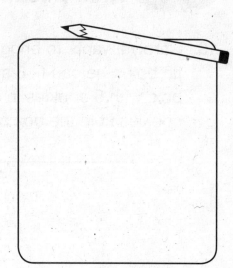

17. Suzy the Frog sits on the number 500 on a number line. Suzy hops forward 8 times, moving 100 spaces to the right each time. On which number does Suzy finally rest?

_____

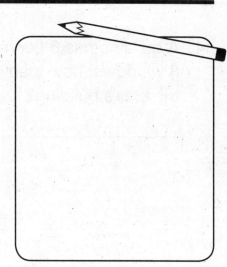

18. Al has 523 trading cards. Suppose 4 other children also have 523 cards each. About how many cards do the children have altogether?

_____

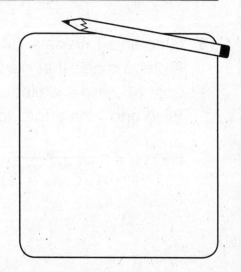

Chapter 7 **Multiplication**

19. The sum of Jana's age and Carina's age is 17. Carina is 1 year older than Jana. What number represents the product of their ages?

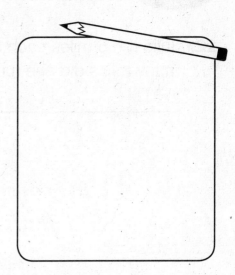

_____

20. In 6 years Allan will be 3 times as old as he is now. How old will Allan be in 6 years?

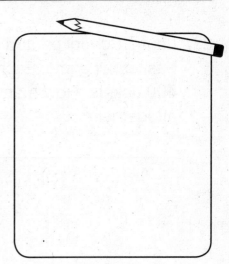

_____

21. Jackie and her baby brother are building towers out of blocks. They have each used 47 blocks in their tower. How many blocks have they used?

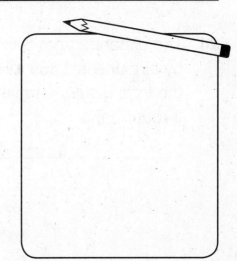

_____

Chapter 7 Multiplication

22. Julie ran 5 miles each day for 5 days. How many miles did she run in all?

_____

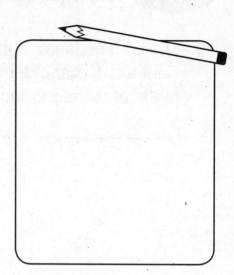

23. Laurel School printed 3,000 tickets for a basketball game. Each of 6 classes has sold 400 tickets. How many tickets have they sold altogether?

_____

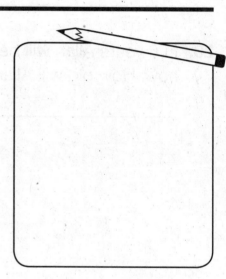

24. The distance from San Francisco to Chicago by airplane is 1,859 miles one way. Estimate the total distance traveled by a plane making 3 round trips.

_____

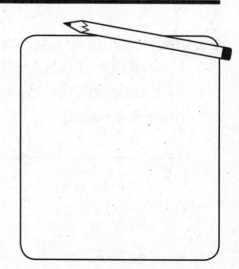

Chapter 7 Multiplication

25. One company packs an average of 300 peanuts in each bag. About how many peanuts are in a case of 80 bags?

_____

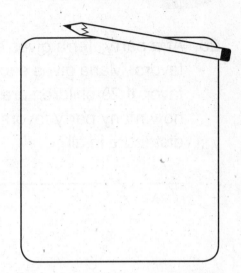

26. Each passenger on an airplane carries 101 pounds of luggage. There are 84 passengers on the flight, and the weight capacity of the luggage compartment is 10,000 pounds. How many pounds of luggage capacity are unused?

_____

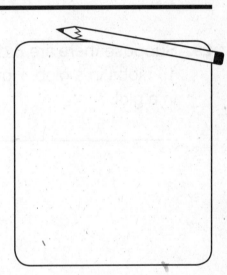

27. Salinda, Vicente, and Michelle shared a box of peanuts. Each person received 23 peanuts, and there were 2 peanuts left. How many peanuts were in the box?

_____

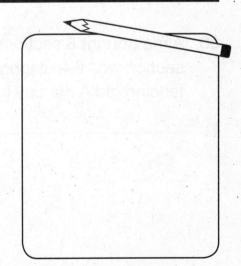

Chapter 7 **Multiplication**

28. At a party, Terra gives each guest 2 party favors. Maria gives each guest another party favor. If 25 children are guests at the party, how many party favors do Terra and Maria distribute in all?

_____

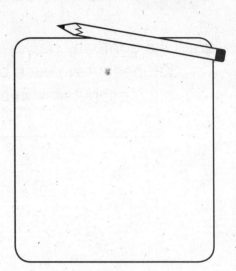

29. Suppose there are 8 drops of ink in a blob and 15 blobs in a glob. How many drops of ink are in a glob?

_____

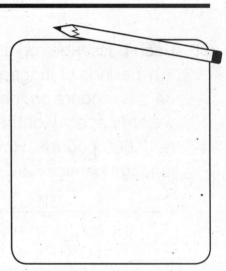

30. Alma bought 8 sections of fencing. Each section was 6 feet long. How many feet of fencing did Alma buy in all?

_____

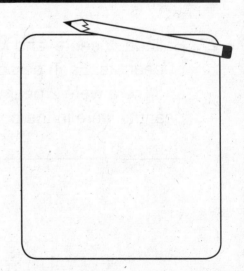

Chapter 8 Division

1. Troy sold 5 trading cards. Now Troy has 16 trading cards, which is twice as many cards as Alexander has. How many trading cards does Alexander have?

_____

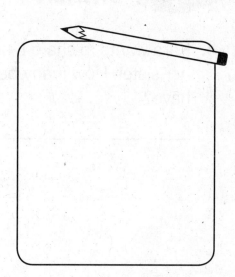

2. Karen has 20 ounces of apple juice. How many juice glasses can she fill if each glass holds 5 ounces of juice?

_____

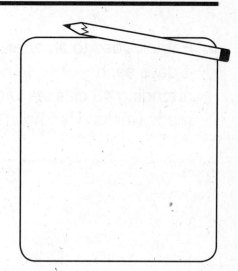

3. Four friends have a box of cookies. There are 24 cookies in the box, and they decide to share the cookies equally. How many cookies does each friend receive?

_____

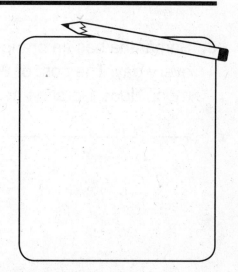

Chapter 8 **Division**

4. Kara wants to share 8 hair barrettes equally with her sister. How many barrettes will each girl have?

_____

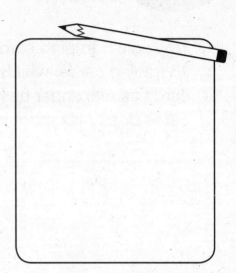

5. Patrick goes to an after-school reading program 4 days each week. He receives an award for attending 48 classes without an absence. How many weeks does he attend?

_____

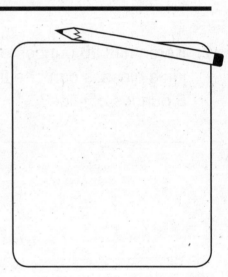

6. Samantha has an orange with her breakfast every day. The cost of 8 oranges is $2.00. How much does 1 orange cost?

_____

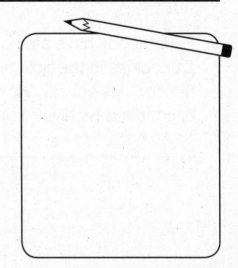

Chapter 8 **Division**

7. Tang and Jeni have a bag of cookies. There are 36 cookies, and they want to divide them evenly. How many cookies will they each have?

_____

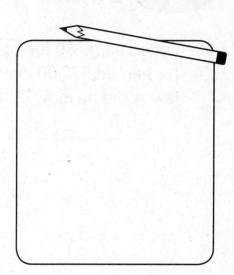

8. Joel and Howard catch 17 fish on Monday, 8 fish on Tuesday, 13 fish on Thursday, and 14 fish on Saturday. On which days are they able to share the fish equally?

_____

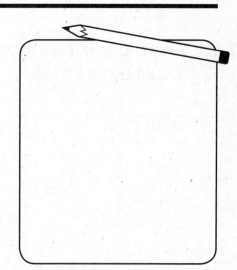

9. Javier, Leah, Rafi, and Sue are at the amusement park. They each buy 12 ride tickets. The roller coaster costs 4 tickets, and the tilt-a-whirl costs 3 tickets. How many rides can Sue take on the tilt-a-whirl?

_____

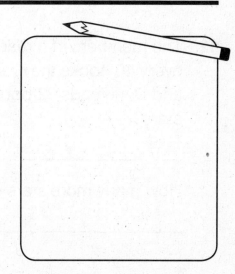

Chapter 8 **Division**

10. Jaden earns $9 for each lawn that he mows. He earned $72.00 last weekend. How many lawns did he mow?

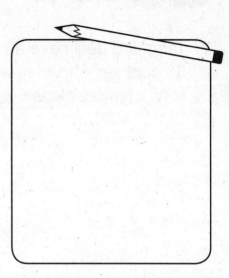

_____

11. Starting at 0, how many steps will it take you to count by 9s to 45?

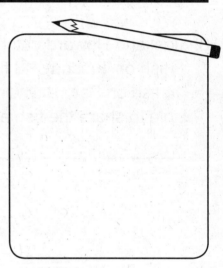

_____

12. The members of a reading club get 1 star for every 10 books they read. Avi reads 40 books, and Dani reads 32 books. Who has more stars?

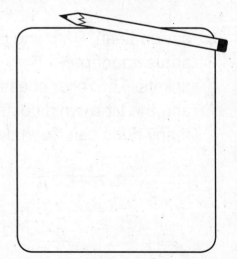

_____

How many more stars does this person have?

_____

Chapter 8 **Division**

13. The fine for an overdue book at the public library is 5¢ a day. Dailon returns his books 1 day late. He pays a 45¢ fine. How many books does he return?

_____

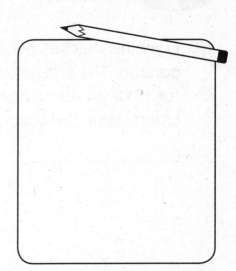

14. Jim, Debbie, and Becky are sharing a book. Jim and Debbie each get the book for 2 days of the week. Becky gets the book the rest of the week. Is this equal sharing?

_____

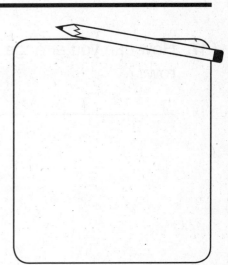

15. A bookshelf has 8 shelves that can each hold 20 books of the same size. If you place 100 books on the bookshelf, starting with the top shelf and moving down, how many shelves can you fill completely?

_____

How many shelves will be completely empty?

_____

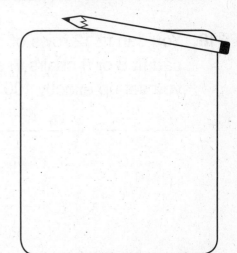

Chapter 8 **Division**

16. Francine watches her caterpillar build a cocoon. The caterpillar is inside the cocoon for 19 days. About how many weeks is the caterpillar in the cocoon?

_____

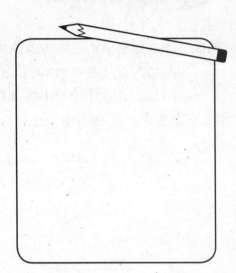

17. How can you arrange 24 counters in 4 equal rows?

_____

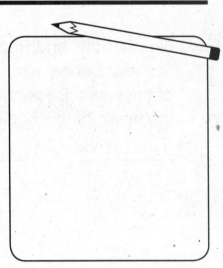

18. You can fit 12 rows of chairs in a room. You can fit 8 or 9 chairs in each row. How would you set up exactly 100 chairs?

_____

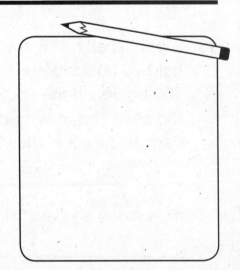

Chapter 8 **Division**

19. Estimate the number of times you would
see the number 7 in the page numbers of a
100-page mystery book.

_____

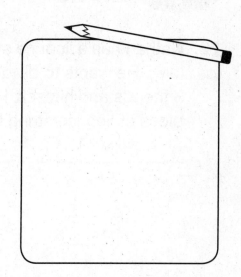

20. Liz got a bead kit for her birthday with
12 different kinds of beads in it. If the whole
kit has 108 beads, how many of each kind
are there?

_____

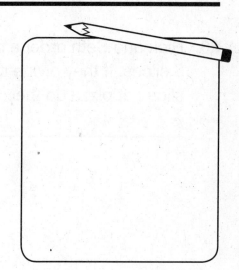

21. What is the least whole number that is divisible
by all of the numbers 1 through 4?

_____

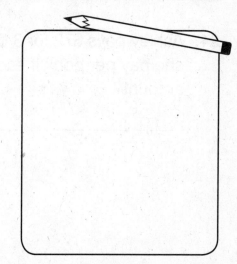

Chapter 8 **Division**

22. Nathan has a licorice string that is 24 inches long. He wants to divide it equally among his 3 friends and himself. How long should each piece of licorice string be?

_____

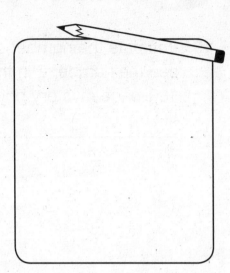

23. Rick and Seth order a pizza that is cut into 8 slices. If they divide it equally, how many slices of pizza do they each get?

_____

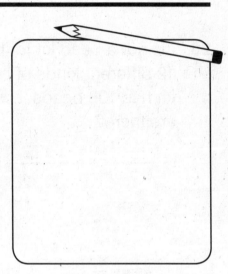

24. Ashley pays $72 for 3 books. How much does she pay per book if each book costs the same amount?

_____

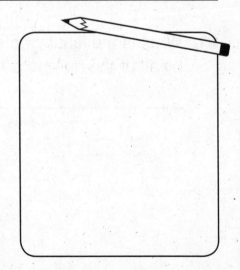

Chapter 8 Division

25. Josef had bowling scores of 112, 121, and 118. What was Josef's average score?

_____

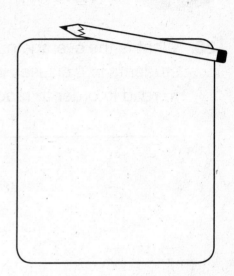

26. Four friends rented 3 videos for $9.00 and purchased snacks and drinks for $7.80. The total cost was shared equally. What was the cost per person?

_____

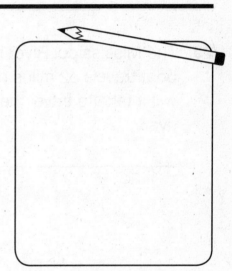

27. How many different ways can 24 objects be divided into 1 or more equal groups with no objects left over?

_____

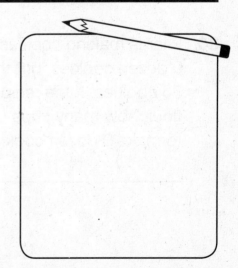

Chapter 8 **Division**

28. What is the average number of books the students in 4 classes in a school would need to read in order to read 2,000 books?

_____

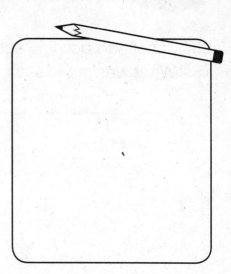

29. The Mississippi River is 2,340 miles long. If a boat travels 52 miles per day, how many days will it take to travel the complete length of the river?

_____

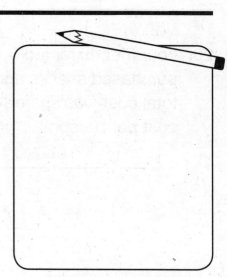

30. Pilar is making cookies. She wants to make 9 dozen cookies, but the recipe makes only 36 cookies. If the recipe requires 3 cups of flour, how many cups of flour does Pilar need to make 9 dozen cookies?

_____

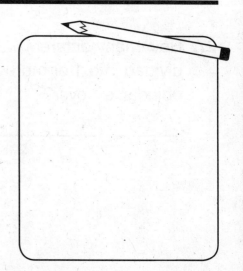

Chapter 9   Geometry

1. Look at the letters below. How many line segments do the letters have?

M Z K A Y W

M: _____   A: _____

Z: _____   Y: _____

K: _____   W: _____

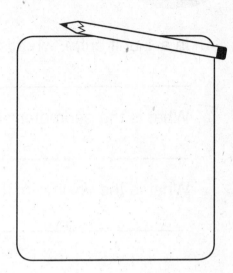

2. Kristal is showing her friends a math magic trick. She says she can draw 2 straight lines in a square and make 6 triangles, without cutting the square. Draw a picture to show how Kristal does this.

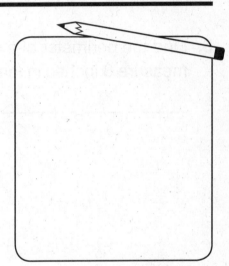

3. Draw a rectangle that is 3 units wide and 4 units long. In how many different ways can you divide the rectangle into 2 congruent parts by drawing 1 line?

_____

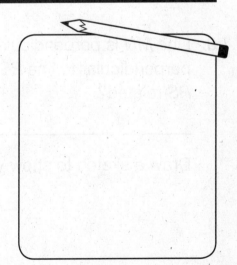

Chapter 9 **Geometry**

4. In a 1-unit cube, what is the area of the top?

_____

What is the perimeter of the top?

_____

What is the volume of the cube?

_____

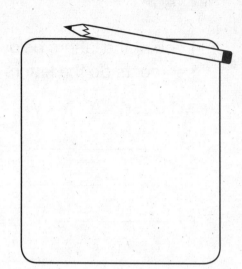

5. Find the perimeter of a square whose sides measure 8 inches in length.

_____

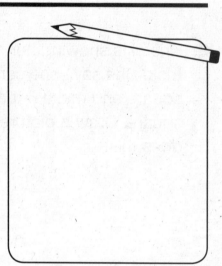

6. Line *MN* is perpendicular to line *PQ*. Line *PQ* is perpendicular to line *RS*. How are lines *MN* and *RS* related?

_____

Draw a sketch to show your answer.

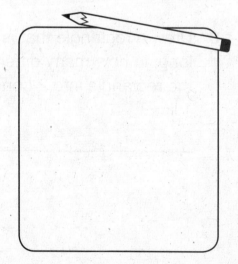

Chapter 9 **Geometry**

7. In which shape—a rectangle or a square—are the 2 diagonals always perpendicular?

_____

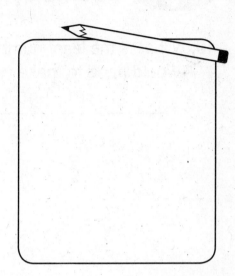

8. Draw a square and its diagonals. How many different triangles exist inside the square?

_____

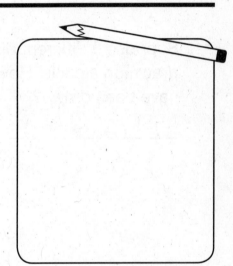

9. What is the least number of times you need to fold a circle to divide the circle into 8 equal parts?

_____

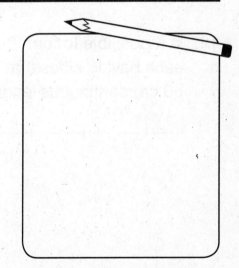

Chapter 9 **Geometry**

10. What is the least number of line segments you would need to make two triangles?

_____

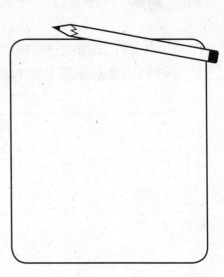

11. Suppose 3 different diameters have been drawn on a circle. How many different radii have been drawn?

_____

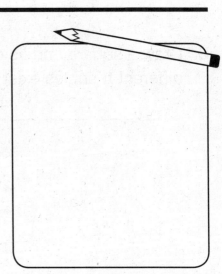

12. Is it possible to form 2 equilateral triangles, each having sides that measure 12 cm, from a 60 cm continuous length of wire?

_____

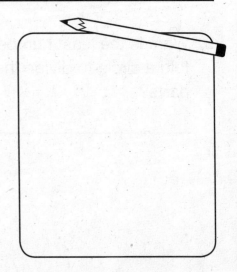

Chapter 10 Data and Probability

1. On each side of a street there are 5 houses. The house numbers on one side of the street are 1501, 1503, 1505, 1507, and 1509. What might 5 of the house numbers on the opposite side of the street be?

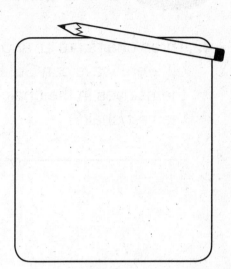

_____

---

2. Look at these two 4-digit numbers:

3,456 and 3,443

For each number, explain the digit pattern.

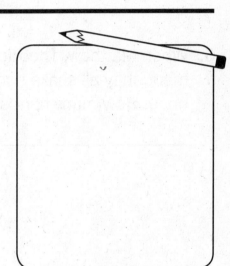

_____

_____

---

3. The books in a bookcase are arranged in a pattern. The first shelf has 1 book, the second shelf has 5 books, the third shelf has 9 books, and the fifth shelf has 17 books. How many books are likely to be on the fourth shelf?

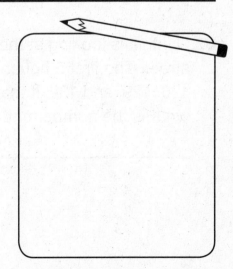

_____

Name _____ Date _____

4. Three chairs are arranged in a row. How many different ways can Su, Ken, and Cristina seat themselves in the chairs if Cristina always sits in the first chair?

_____

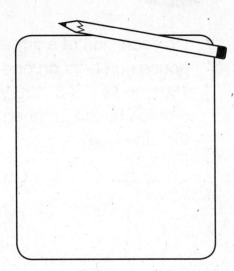

5. When Matthew, Theodore, Sandy, and Carole meet, they all shake hands with each other once. How many handshakes are there?

_____

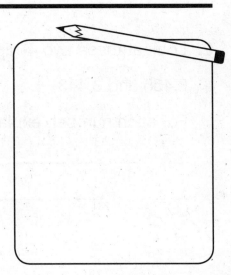

6. Cynthia is looking at the house numbers on her street. The first 5 house numbers are 120, 123, 126, 129, and 132. If that pattern continues, what is the number of the tenth house?

_____

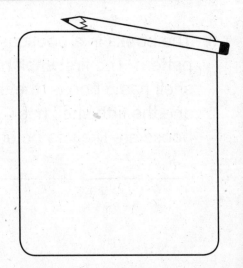

Chapter 10 **Data and Probability**

7. Tito, Joey, Shannon, and Trina ran a race. Tito finished before Joey but after Trina. Shannon finished last. List the racers in order from first to last.

_____

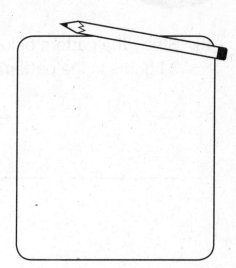

8. Joshua is making a picture by choosing one shape, one size, and one color from the list below. List all the possible combinations he can use to make his picture.

Shape: square, rectangle, or triangle
Size: large or small
Color: blue or yellow

_____

_____

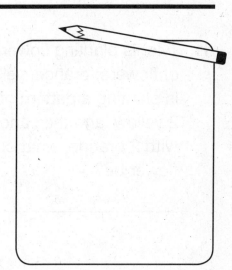

9. Gina is making a necklace out of beads for her mother. She uses a pattern of 2 red, 2 white, 2 pink, 2 white. How many white beads does she need if she uses 16 red beads?

_____

How many pink beads does she need?

_____

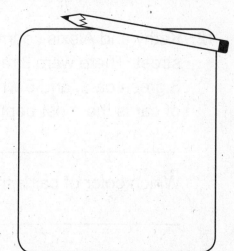

Chapter 10 **Data and Probability**

10. Study the pattern below. Draw the next 3 figures in the pattern.

_____   _____   _____

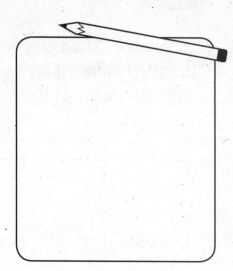

11. Tyler is planting flowers. He has 3 colors of flowers: orange, yellow, and white. Tyler is planting a pattern of 2 orange, 1 white, 2 yellow, and then another white. If he starts with 2 orange, what color should the tenth flower be?

_____

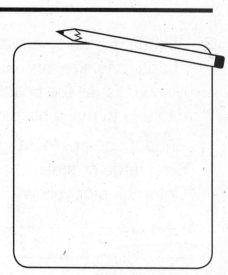

12. Kathy and Alexis counted cars parked on their street. There were 8 red cars, 4 blue cars, 3 green cars, and 5 white cars. Which color of car is the most popular?

_____

Which color of car is the least popular?

_____

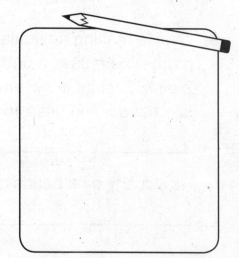

Chapter 10 Data and Probability

13. Ramiro eats a peanut butter and jelly sandwich 3 days a week. Once a week he eats a ham sandwich, and once a week he eats a roast beef sandwich. Which kind of sandwich is he most likely to eat?

_____

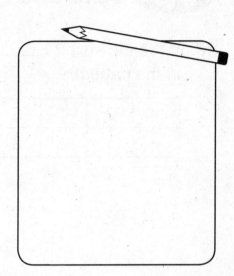

14. There are 8 cookies in a cookie jar. Of those, 4 are chocolate chip, 3 are peanut butter, and 1 is a sugar cookie. If you pull 1 cookie out at random, which type of cookie are you least likely to pick?

_____

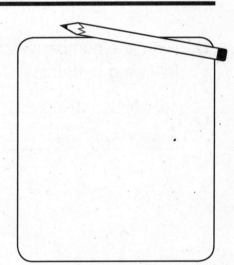

15. A spinner has 5 equal sections marked with the numbers 1 through 5. What is the probability of landing on an odd number?

_____

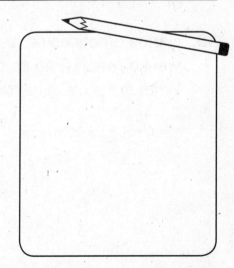

Chapter 10 **Data and Probability**

16. Write the next 2 *x* terms and the next 2 *y* terms in the pattern.

x	2	4	6	8	10		
y	1	2	3	4	5		

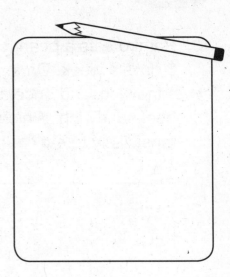

17. Write the numbers that will complete the following patterns.

10, 20, 30, 40, 50, _____, _____, . . .

0, 150, 300, 450, _____, 750, _____, . . .

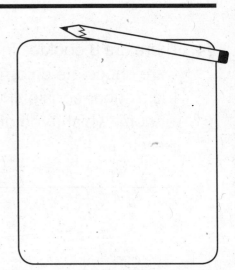

18. Carlos practices on his guitar for 1 hour each weekday and 2 hours each weekend day. Write the pattern he follows.

_____

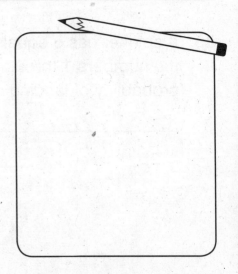

Chapter 10 **Data and Probability**

19. Find the mean, median, mode, and range for the data set below.

1, 2, 2, 2, 2, 3

mean: _____   mode: _____

median: _____   range: _____

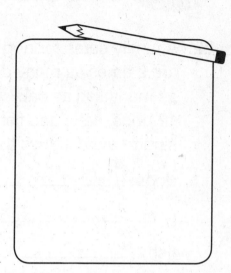

---

20. Four students are waiting in line at the water fountain. As they wait, how many different ways can they arrange themselves in line if Jamaal is always first?

_____

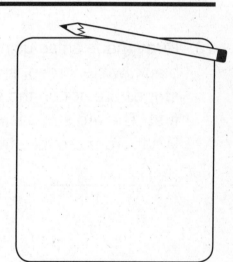

---

21. A fence around a square enclosure must be supported by 3 fence posts on each side. What is the least number of fence posts that can be used to support the fence?

_____

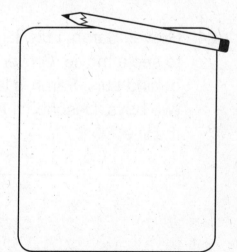

Chapter 10 **Data and Probability**

22. A family cares for dogs, cats, and fish. There are 2 times as many dogs as cats and 3 times as many fish as cats. Altogether, the family has 12 dogs, cats, and fish. How many of each kind of animal does the family care for?

dogs: _____

cats: _____

fish: _____

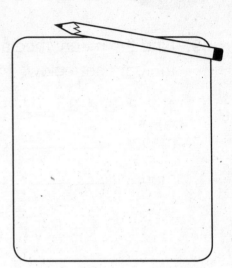

23. Rudy made a flag using 4 vertical stripes— black, white, green, and red. The red and black stripes are not on the ends. The green stripe is first. The red stripe is next to the white stripe. What order are the stripes in?

_____

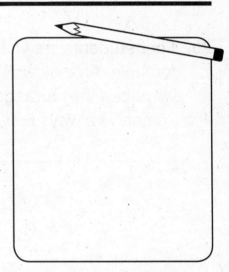

24. Grover, Sarah, Luis, Linda, and Nina are in line to see a movie. Grover is in front of Nina but behind Luis. Sarah is last. Linda is in front of two boys. Describe the order of the people in the line.

_____

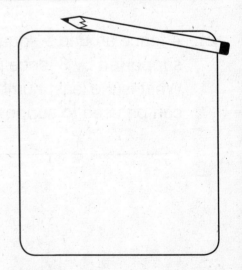

Chapter 10 **Data and Probability**

25. The house numbers on one side of a street are even numbers from 138 to 152. How many houses are on that side of the street?

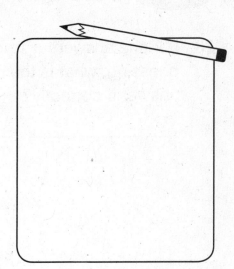

_____

26. Three books are on a shelf. In how many different ways can you arrange them?

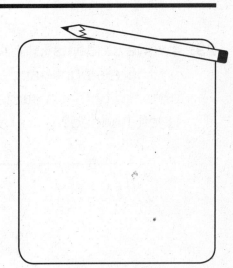

_____

27. Suppose you reach into a bag that contains 4 red and 7 green marbles. What is the probability you select a red marble?

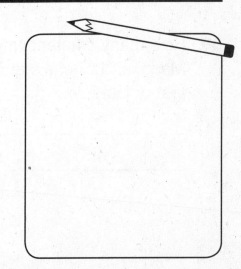

_____

Chapter 10 **Data and Probability**

28. If Alana answers a True or False question by guessing, what is the probability she will answer it correctly?

_____

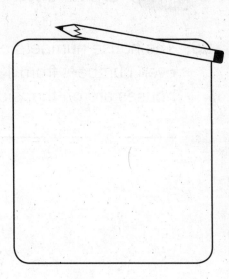

29. Twelve students in a class are left-handed, and 15 are right-handed. What is the probability that a student chosen at random is left-handed?

_____

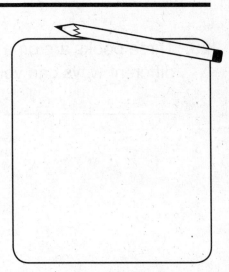

30. How many different ways can Lucia, Irene, Mario, and Cherie stand in line if Irene is either first or last?

_____

_____

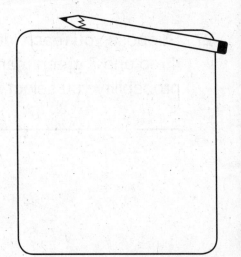

Name _____   Date _____

1. Michael charges $10 to walk a dog for $\frac{1}{2}$ hour. Margie charges $17 to walk a dog for 45 minutes. If a customer wants her dog walked for $1\frac{1}{2}$ hours, who should she hire if she wants to pay the least amount of money?

   _____

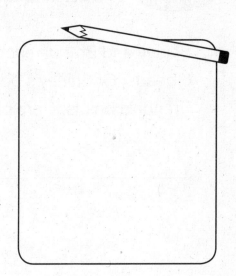

2. Simon and Todd cut a sandwich into equal pieces. They decide to share the sandwich equally with friends. How much of the total sandwich will Simon and Todd eat if 2 friends join them?

   _____

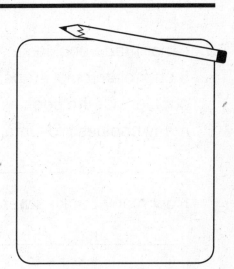

3. Manuel had a box of treats for his dogs. Fluffy ate $\frac{3}{12}$ of the treats, Sport ate $\frac{7}{12}$ of the treats, and Fido ate $\frac{2}{12}$ of the treats. Which dog ate the greatest number of treats?

   _____

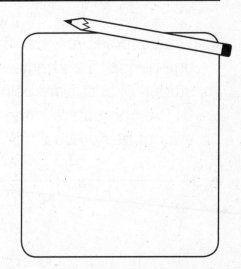

Chapter 11 **Fractions and Mixed Numbers**

4. Shirley and Brenda each make bracelets out of 6 beads. Of Shirley's beads, $\frac{5}{6}$ are pink. Of Brenda's beads, $\frac{2}{6}$ are pink. Who uses the most pink beads?

_____

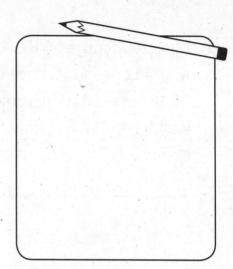

5. Omar made cookies for his class. He made 8 chocolate chip, 10 peanut butter, and 6 sugar cookies. Of the cookies, $\frac{1}{4}$ were not eaten. How many cookies did Omar make?

_____

How many cookies were not eaten?

_____

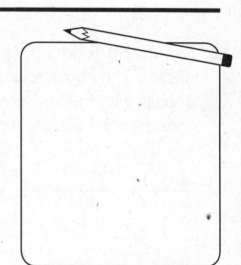

6. The school library has 8 computers. During one period, 5 computers are being used by students, and 2 are being used by teachers. Of the computers in the library, what fraction are not being used?

_____

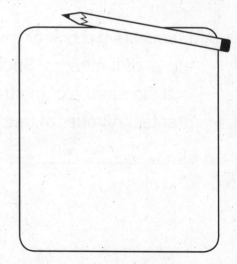

80

Chapter 11
Fractions and Mixed Numbers

7. In the cafeteria, each pizza is cut into 8 equal pieces. Yesterday the cafeteria served 38 slices of pizza. What improper fraction tells what amount of pizzas were served?

_____

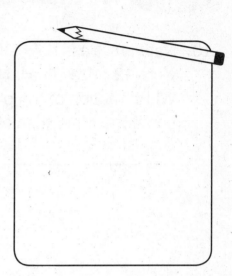

8. Last week Zeke read $\frac{1}{2}$ of a book. This week he read $\frac{3}{8}$ of the book. During which week did he read more of the book?

_____

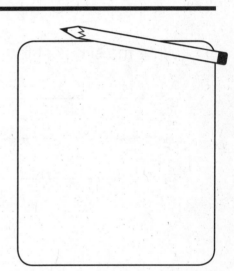

9. Gary has $\frac{2}{5}$ of a dollar in his pocket. How many oranges can Gary buy if oranges cost 20¢ each?

_____

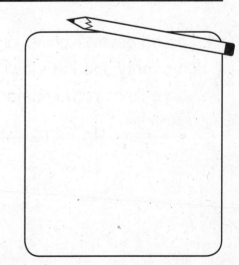

Chapter 11 **Fractions and Mixed Numbers**

10. Natalie's class held a fundraising raffle. There were 12 prizes in all. Natalie won 2 prizes. What fraction of the prizes were won by someone other than Natalie?

_____

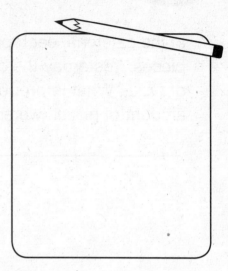

11. Write the simplest form of each fraction.

$\frac{3}{6}$ = _____ $\frac{3}{24}$ = _____

$\frac{5}{20}$ = _____ $\frac{2}{20}$ = _____

$\frac{2}{12}$ = _____ $\frac{5}{60}$ = _____

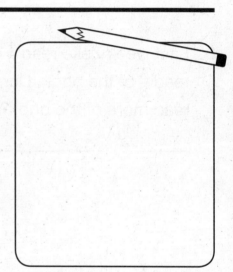

12. Jared gave 12 coins, or $\frac{1}{4}$ of his collection, to a charity auction. How many coins were in Jared's collection before he gave some away?

_____

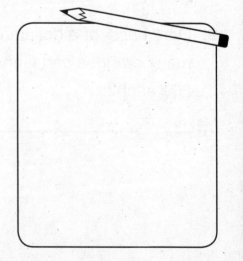

Chapter 11 **Fractions and Mixed Numbers**

13. Alice finds 9 dimes under the cushion of a chair. What fraction of 1 dollar does she find?

_____

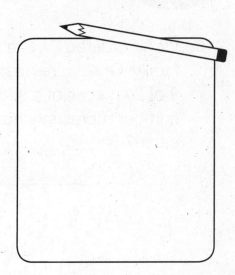

14. Dave needs 2 pieces of string for an art project. The first must be $\frac{9}{16}$ inch long, and the second must be $\frac{11}{16}$ inch long. What length of string does Dave need altogether?

_____

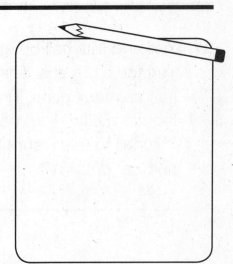

15. Of the students in Tony's class, $\frac{17}{23}$ have dogs, and $\frac{5}{23}$ have cats. The rest of the students don't have pets. What fraction of the students do not have pets?

_____

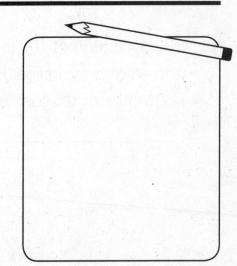

Chapter 11 **Fractions and Mixed Numbers**

16. Victor ordered 2 vegetarian pizzas for his family. One entire pizza was eaten, along with 9 of 24 pieces of a second pizza. What mixed number represents how much pizza was eaten?

_____,_____

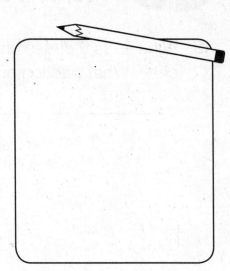

17. Yuri and Mitchell bought a package of pens. Yuri took 12 pens. That left Mitchell with only half as many pens. They decided to share them equally. How many pens did Yuri give to Mitchell to make sure they each got the same number of pens?

_____

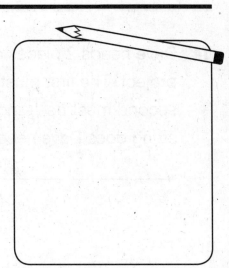

18. In a collection of 104 insects, $\frac{1}{2}$ are moths and $\frac{1}{4}$ are dragonflies. How many insects are not moths or dragonflies?

_____

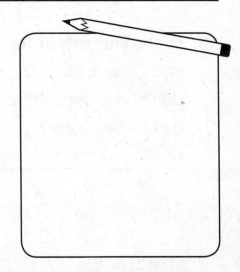

Chapter 11 **Fractions and Mixed Numbers**

19. Brittany's class sells magazines as a fundraiser. For each magazine that is sold, Brittany's class keeps a quarter of the sale price. Brittany's dad purchased $92.00 worth of magazines. How much money does Brittany's class keep from his purchase?

_____

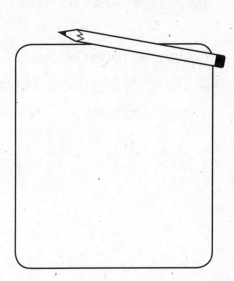

20. Suppose a canoe can be rented for $4 an hour. At that rate, what would be the cost of renting the canoe for $3\frac{1}{2}$ hours?

_____

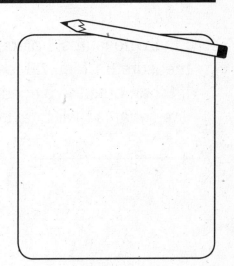

21. What fraction of a mile is 880 yards?

_____

What fraction of a mile is 440 yards?

_____

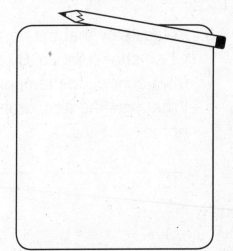

Name _____ Date _____

1. Janelle received a score of $\frac{75}{100}$ on her math test. Rianne received a score of 0.85. Who got the better score?

   _____

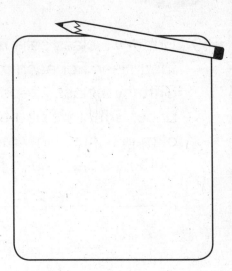

2. Ethan measures 3 pieces of lumber. They measure 8.1 feet, 7.8 feet, and 9.8 feet in length. If Ethan puts the pieces of lumber in a straight line, what is their total length?

   _____

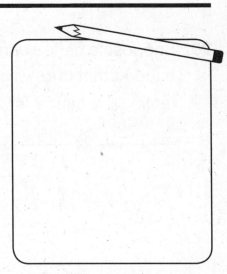

3. Kelsey saw that the temperature was 42.5°F when she woke up. By the time she got home from school, the temperature had dropped 7.1°F. What was the temperature when Kelsey got home?

   _____

Chapter 12 **Decimals**

4. Carla made trail mix with 1.25 pounds of peanuts, 1.5 pounds of walnuts, 0.8 pound of almonds, and 2.2 pounds of raisins. What was the weight of the trail mix when Carla finished mixing the ingredients?

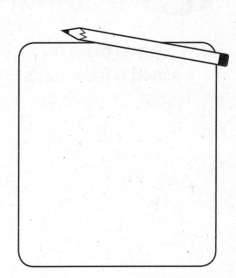

_____

5. Martina and Angelo ran in the same 10-kilometer race. Martina finished the race in 53.24 minutes. Angelo finished the race in 37.09 minutes. How much faster did Angelo complete the race?

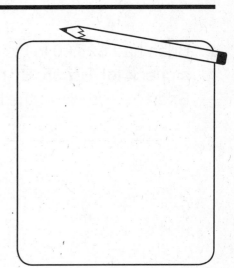

_____

6. Out of 100 cupcakes at a bakery, $\frac{27}{100}$ cupcakes are white cake with chocolate frosting. How is that fraction written as a decimal number?

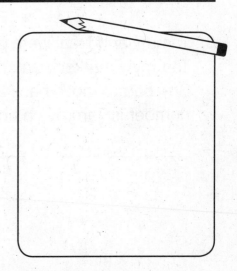

_____

87

Name _____ Date _____

1. A football player ran 7 yards and then was pushed back 4 yards. What was the total number of yards the player gained?

_____

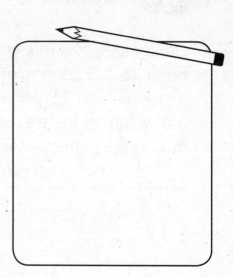

2. Brian had $25.00 in his bank account. He wrote a check for $27.35. By how much money was Brian overdrawn at the bank?

_____

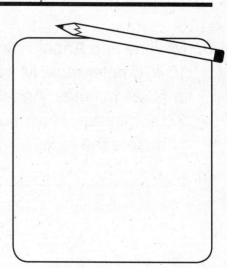

3. Tammy and Neal were playing a board game. Tammy's marker was on square number 12. She had to move back 21 spaces. What square number is Tammy on now?

_____

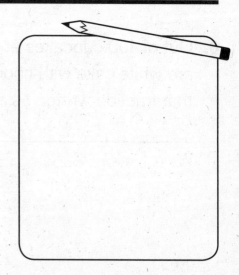

Name _____ Date _____

4. Juno is on ⁻16 on a number line. If he adds 12, what number will he be on?

_____

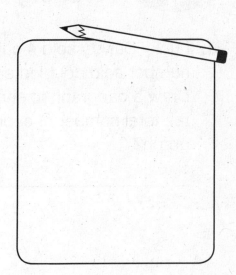

_____

5. The temperature on the thermometer reads ⁻12°F. What is the temperature after it rises 24 degrees?

_____

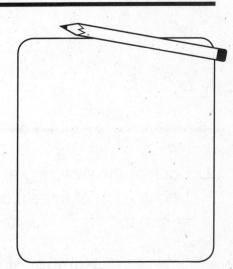

6. Begin at ⁺15 on a number line, and then move 18 units to the left. At what number should you stop?

_____

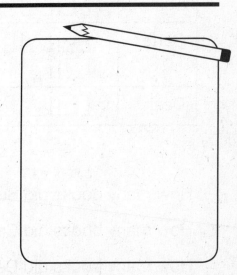

Chapter 14 **Graphing**

1. Lucky Bakery sold 4 cupcakes on Monday. The number sold doubled each day through Friday. Draw a bar graph to show these data. What is the total number of cupcakes shown on the graph?

   _____

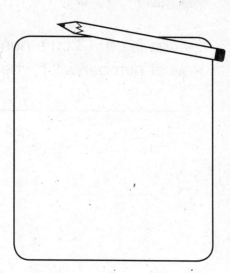

2. Look at the picture graph. It shows how many books each of three students read over the summer.

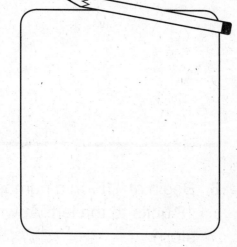

Number of Books Read

Suki	📖 📖 📖 📖 📖
Carter	📖 📖 📖 📖 📖 📖 📖 📖 📖
Dean	📖 📖 📖 📖

📖 = 2 books

How many books did Suki read? _____

How many books did Carter read? _____

How many books did Dean read? _____

Chapter 14   # Graphing

3. Pablo used a line graph to show the number of kites that his father's store sold over a 3-month period.

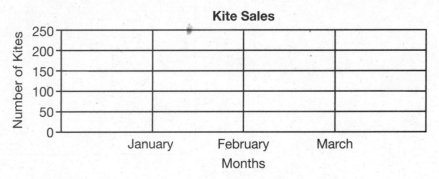

Kite Sales

January	100
February	50
March	150

Use the data to complete the line graph.

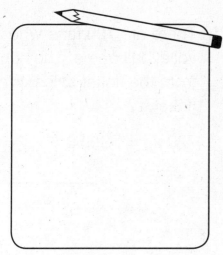

4. Marla made a circle graph to show the kinds of things her school recycles. She discovered that 50% of the materials were paper, 25% were plastic, and 25% were metal. Divide and label the circle to graph the data.

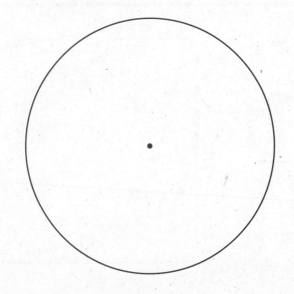

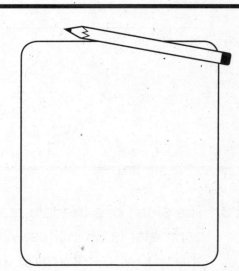

Chapter 15 **Algebra**

1. There are 720 fans who buy tickets to a volleyball game. The school makes $2,880 from the ticket sales. What is the cost of each ticket, *t*?

    720 x *t* = $2,880

    t = _____

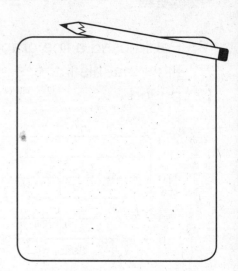

2. Troy was born in 1999. Grandfather was born in 1957. Write an equation to show how to figure out how old Grandfather was when Troy was born.

    _____

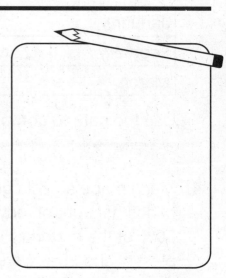

3. The sides of a triangle are the same length. The perimeter is 36 inches. Write an equation to show how to determine the length of each side. Let *s* stand for the length of each side.

    _____

    What is the length of each side?

    _____

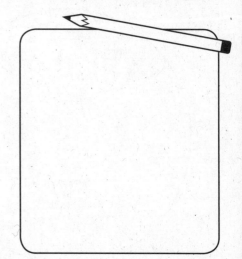

Chapter 15 **Algebra**

4. There are 27 students in each fourth grade class. The school has a total of 135 fourth grade students. Let *n* stand for the number of fourth grade classes. Write an equation that shows how to find out how many fourth grade classes there are.

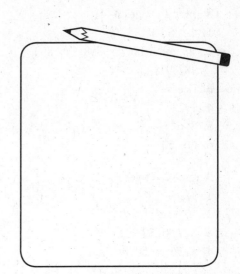

_____

How many fourth grade classes are there?

_____

5. Shelley and Andrew earn $12 for each yard that they mow. Last month, they mowed 15 yards. Write an equation that shows how to figure out how much Shelley and Andrew earned last month.

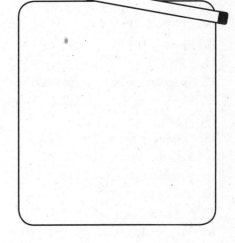

_____

How much money did they earn?

_____

Write an equation to show how to figure out how much each person got if they divided the money equally.

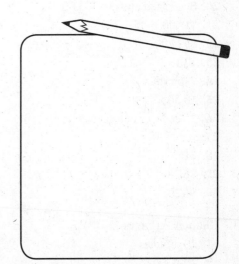

_____

How much did each person earn?

_____

Answer Key

Chapter 1 (Pages 3–4)

1. 4,826 + 9,184
2. six numbers; 789, 798, 879, 897, 987, 978
3. Leesa
4. 1978
5. 8; 6
6. 60,057

Chapter 2 (Pages 5–14)

1. Mark
2. 70 cents; $1.30
3. $27.50; $28.49
4. $1.75; $7.50; 40 days
5. Paula: $2.00; Steven: $1.60; Paula
6. 7 dimes; 3 quarters
7. $5.00; $2.50
8. Suggested answer: About $11.00
9. $2.35; no
10. Kevin
11. $50; $50
12. Suggested answer: About $4.00
13. $1.55; more than one dollar
14. $7.00
15. Possible answers: four $1 bills, 3 quarters; three $1 bills, 6 quarters, 2 dimes, 1 nickel
16. Mrs. Wong; $122
17. 5 quarters
18. Suggested answer: About $11.00
19. $38.64
20. Suggested answer: $45.00
21. $14.00
22. $324.00
23. $3.17
24. 7 quarters
25. $3.50
26. 25 cents or one quarter
27. yes
28. $15
29. $6.28
30. $1.20

Chapter 3 (Pages 15–18)

1. 20 minutes
2. 4:00 P.M.
3. one train; two trains
4. 3:00 P.M.; Tim
5. Answers will vary.
6. 55 minutes
7. 4:35 P.M.
8. 15 times
9. Wednesday; April 28
10. 12 minutes
11. 7 hours
12. September 22

Chapter 4 (Pages 19–26)

1. 16
2. 73 cookies
3. 38 lures
4. 32 ribbons
5. 957 cans
6. 211 pounds
7. 6 blocks
8. 225 yards
9. 35 outlets
10. 70
11. 47
12. 37 goals
13. Suggested answer: About 50,000 seats
14. 4,436 miles
15. 21 years old
16. no
17. 28 photographs
18. 1,363 birds
19. 23,408 items
20. Suggested answer: About 18,000 miles
21. 27 miles
22. 17 inches; 20 inches
23. Suggested answer: About 1,100 miles
24. Suggested answer: About 2,000 miles

Chapter 5 (Pages 27–36)

1. 52
2. 19 books
3. 5 sweaters
4. 7 stamping blocks
5. 8 yards
6. 55 words per minute
7. Kayla; 2 more seashells
8. 89 pennies more
9. 65 pennies fewer
10. 9 more stickers
11. 112 beads
12. 12 extra hot dog buns
13. Ms. Estrada: 35; Mrs. Nelson: 32
14. 186 people
15. 3 cans
16. 22 buttons
17. 26
18. 643 – 267 = 376 or 643 – 376 = 267; Correct as is. 1,173 – 556 = 614 or 1,173 – 714 = 459; The sum is not correct. It should be 1,273. 1,289 – 491 = 798 or 1,289 – 758 = 531; The sum is not correct. It should be 1,249.
19. 119 eggs
20. No. He has only 27,000 miles.
21. 7
22. 31,473 apples
23. 19
24. 4 cents more
25. 75 years old
26. 147
27. 7
28. back 3
29. 140 students
30. 10th floor

Chapter 6 (Pages 37–44)

1. Answers will vary.
2. 4 cups; 8 cups
3. 2 quarts or $\frac{1}{2}$ gallon
4. 11°F; increase
5. Both hold the same amount of water.
6. Kendra; 250 mL more
7. 24°F
8. no
9. 10 cups
10. 28 feet
11. 27 cm; 72 cm

12. 750 feet
13. 75 grams
14. 29°F colder
15. 1,291 feet
16. 17 inches
17. Suggested answer:
    About 3,200,000 acres
18. 218 bricks
19. 4 units
20. 8 cm
21. The area of the right triangle is $\frac{1}{2}$ the area of the rectangle.
22. 37 inches³
23. 59°F
24. 37 inches

Chapter 7 (Pages 45–54)
1. 10 more water glasses
2. 12 erasers
3. $15
4. 18 times
5. Julia; 1 sticker
6. 5 more letters than packages
7. 20 students
8. 20 storybooks
9. 30 trading cards
10. 35 eggs
11. 22 cards
12. $1.00
13. 40 cookies
14. 48 windows
15. flowers
16. 65
17. 1,300
18. Suggested answer:
    About 2,500 cards
19. 72
20. 9 years old
21. 94 blocks
22. 25 miles
23. 2,400 tickets
24. Suggested answer:
    About 12,000 miles
25. Suggested answer:
    About 24,000 peanuts
26. 1,516 pounds

27. 71 peanuts
28. 75 party favors
29. 120 drops of ink
30. 48 feet

Chapter 8 (Pages 55–64)
1. 8 trading cards
2. 4 juice glasses
3. 6 cookies
4. 4 barrettes
5. 12 weeks
6. $0.25
7. 18 cookies
8. Tuesday and Saturday
9. 4 rides
10. 8 lawns
11. 5 steps
12. Avi
13. 9 books
14. no
15. 5 shelves; 3 shelves
16. Suggested answer:
    About 3 weeks
17. 6 counters in each of 4 rows
18. Answers will vary. Possible
    answer: 8 chairs in 8 rows and 9
    chairs in 4 rows
19. Suggested answer:
    About 20 times
20. 9 beads of each kind
21. 12
22. 6 inches
23. 4 slices
24. $24
25. 117
26. $4.20
27. 8 ways
28. 500 books per class
29. 45 days
30. 9 cups

Chapter 9 (pages 65–68)
1. M: 4 line segments
   Z: 3 line segments
   K: 3 line segments
   A: 3 line segments

Y: 3 line segments
W: 4 line segments
2. Students should draw two
   diagonal segments, from corner
   to corner.
3. 4 ways
4. 1 square unit; 4 units;
   1 cubic unit
5. $P = 32$ inches
6. The lines are parallel.
7. square
8. 8 triangles
9. 3 times
10. 4 line segments
11. 6 radii
12. yes

Chapter 10 (Pages 69–78)
1. Suggested answers: 1502, 1504,
   1506, 1508, 1510
2. Possible answer: 3,456: Each
   digit is 1 more than the previous
   digit; 3,443: The order of the
   first two digits is in the opposite
   order of the second two digits.
3. 13 books
4. 2 ways
5. 6 handshakes
6. 147
7. Trina, Tito, Joey, Shannon
8. large blue square; large blue
   rectangle; large blue triangle;
   small blue square; small blue
   rectangle; small blue triangle;
   large yellow square; large yellow
   rectangle; large yellow triangle;
   small yellow square; small
   yellow rectangle; small yellow
   triangle
9. 32 white beads; 16 pink beads
10.
11. yellow
12. red; green
13. peanut butter and jelly
14. sugar cookie
15. $\frac{1}{3}$

16. $x = 12, 14; y = 6, 7$
17. 60, 70; 600, 900
18. 1, 1, 1; 1, 1, 2, 2
19. mean: 2; median: 2; mode: 2; range: 2
20. 6 ways
21. 8 fence posts
22. dogs: 4; cats: 2; fish: 6
23. green, black, red, white
24. front to back: Linda, Luis, Grover, Nina, Sarah
25. 8 houses
26. 6 ways
27. $\frac{4}{11}$
28. $\frac{1}{2}$
29. $\frac{12}{27}$ or $\frac{4}{9}$
30. 12 ways

Chapter 11 (Pages 79–85)

1. Michael
2. $\frac{2}{4}$ or $\frac{1}{2}$ of the sandwich
3. Sport
4. Shirley
5. 24 cookies; 6 cookies
6. $\frac{1}{8}$
7. $\frac{38}{8}$
8. last week
9. 2 oranges
10. $\frac{10}{12}$ or $\frac{5}{6}$
11. $\frac{3}{6} = \frac{1}{2}$
    $\frac{5}{20} = \frac{1}{4}$
    $\frac{2}{12} = \frac{1}{6}$
    $\frac{3}{24} = \frac{1}{8}$
    $\frac{2}{20} = \frac{1}{10}$
    $\frac{5}{60} = \frac{1}{12}$
12. 48 coins
13. $\frac{90}{100}$ or $\frac{9}{10}$ of a dollar
14. $\frac{20}{16}$ or $1\frac{1}{4}$ inches
15. $\frac{1}{23}$
16. $1\frac{9}{24}$ or $1\frac{3}{8}$

17. 3 pens
18. 26 insects
19. $23.00
20. $14.00
21. $\frac{1}{2}$ mile; $\frac{1}{4}$ mile

Chapter 12 (Pages 86–87)

1. Rianne
2. 25.7 feet
3. 35.4°F
4. 5.75 pounds
5. 16.15 minutes
6. 0.27

Chapter 13 (Pages 88–89)

1. 3
2. $2.35
3. −9
4. −4
5. 12°F
6. −3

Chapter 14 (Pages 90–91)

1. The bars should show 4, 8, 16, 32, and 64 cupcakes. The total is 124 cupcakes.
2. Suki: 10 books; Carter: 18 books; Dean: 8 books
3. The line graph should show that 100 kites were sold in January, 50 were sold in February, and 150 were sold in March.
4. Students should divide the chart into $\frac{1}{2}$, $\frac{1}{4}$, and $\frac{1}{4}$.
   In the $\frac{1}{2}$ section, students should write *Paper;* in one $\frac{1}{4}$ section, students should write *Plastic;* in the other $\frac{1}{4}$ section, students should write *Metal.* Students may also include the percentages in each section.

Chapter 15 (Pages 92–93)

1. $4.00
2. Suggested answer:
   $1999 − 1957 = x$
3. $3 \times s = 36$ inches; s = 12 inches

4. $27 \times n = 135$; 5 fourth grade classes
5. $12 \times 15 = x$; x = $180;
   $180 ÷ 2 = y; y = $90